{百年励志经典}

钻石
就在你身边

[美] 康维尔 / 著   孔瑞华 / 译

中国华侨出版社
·北京·

图书在版编目（CIP）数据

钻石就在你身边/（美）康维尔著；孔瑞华译.—北京：中国华侨出版社，2010．5（2025．5重印）

ISBN 978-7-5113-0411-7

Ⅰ.①钻… Ⅱ.①康… ②孔… Ⅲ.①私人投资—通俗读物 Ⅳ.① F830.59-49

中国版本图书馆 CIP 数据核字（2010）第 081079 号

钻石就在你身边

著　　者：	［美］康维尔
译　　者：	孔瑞华
责任编辑：	王慧玲
责任校对：	胡首一
经　　销：	新华书店
开　　本：	880 毫米 ×1230 毫米　1/32 开　印张：6　字数：120 千字
印　　刷：	河北省三河市天润建兴印务有限公司
版　　次：	2010 年 5 月第 1 版
印　　次：	2025 年 5 月第 2 次印刷
书　　号：	ISBN 978-7-5113-0411-7
定　　价：	39.80 元

中国华侨出版社　北京市朝阳区西坝河东里 77 号楼底商 5 号　邮编：10002
发　行　部：（010）64443051　　　传　真：（010）64439708

如果发现印装质量问题影响阅读，请与印刷厂联系调换。

热卖百年的世界级畅销书(最新译本)

作者介绍

鲁塞·康维尔,被誉为伟大的美国公民。他的演讲稿《钻石就在你身边》曾经在他有生之年被反复演说过6000多次。之后他还用演讲所获得的酬劳建立了一所小的神学院,后来这所神学院发展成了现在的坦普(Temple)大学。这所大学是美国工薪阶层能够上得起的大学之一,它的建成和发展见证了鲁塞·康维尔为自己和别人而活的精彩人生。相应他的这篇演讲稿也在鲁塞·康维尔一次又一次地精彩演说中鼓舞了美国两代人,它真切地向人们表达了一个朴素的道理,那就是能够充分发挥自身才能和资源的人都可以获得成功。而他所留下的《钻石就在你身边》这篇演讲稿正是这个道理的精彩论述,时隔近百年之后,人们依然可以从这篇演讲稿中领会到很多发人深省的道理,而且这些道理都能对人们起着鼓舞人心的作用。

钻石就在你身边

致读者的一封信

亲爱的朋友们：

　　这篇演讲稿是我在这样的情况下构思而成的：每当我要访问某座城市或某个地方时，我都会提前到达那里，然后先去找到当地社区的社长、理发师、旅店老板、学校校长和教堂牧师们了解当地的情况，再进入工厂和商店与当地的人们交谈，而后深入研究当地的环境和人文条件，以便更广泛深入地了解当地的人们在生活中遇到的疑问和面临的困难，当然每个城镇的居民都有不同的问题。接下来我就会有针对性地就他们所共同怀有的疑问发表演说，以此来和居民们共同谈论他们这个地区所关心的话题。《钻石就在你身边》这篇演讲稿所贯穿的主题也是一样，那就是与更多的人一同努力，尽力在我们现有的环境中将自身的能力发挥到最大。

——鲁塞·康维尔

热卖百年的世界级畅销书(最新译本)

TEMPLE 大学为作者所写的墓志铭

对于每一个青年人来说,成功无疑都是一个非常重要的课题。鲁塞·康维尔通过《钻石就在你身边》告诉了我们,成功是一种高尚的追求,热爱金钱并不是罪恶的源泉。如果我们能够用高尚的方式获得成功,那么我们所能为人类创造的贡献就会远远大于我们在穷困的情况下所能做到的。身为牧师的鲁塞·康维尔,曾经在全国各地把这篇稿子演说了6000多次,他把演说所得的报酬400万美元全都用来建造了这所学校。因为他无法忘记自己读大学时的艰辛,所以他毫无保留地用这笔钱资助了很多穷困的高中毕业生,让他们都能够上得起大学。

康维尔几乎每周都要工作七天,每天工作十五六个小时,他的一生都在忘我无私地奉献着,直到他生命的第82个春秋,他为自己所钟爱的事业耗尽了全

钻石就在你身边

部的心血。

在康维尔看来,每一个被上帝带到这个世界上的人,都应该只为一个目的而活,那就是——帮助别人。

康维尔和他的作品《钻石就在你身边》曾经鼓舞了成千上万的美国民众,使他们努力地实现了自己的生活目标,并使美国成为日益强盛的国家。他所传授给人们的这个真理就是:一切美好的事物都在你的身边,就看你是否懂得发挥他们的作用了。时至今日,这位伟大的人道主义者虽然已经远离了我们所生活的时代,但是他所留下的真理却依然有效。或许在我们所生活的环境中,成功的机会并不比在康维尔当时生活的环境中要多,但至少也不会比那时少,因为康维尔曾真诚地告诉过我们,机会就在我们身边,就看我们是否懂得发现。所以,或许已经身为人师、人父、人母的你,在教育下一代时就更应该好好利用这本书。

热卖百年的世界级畅销书（最新译本）

译者推荐语

这是一篇全世界都在看、都在听的演讲稿。它的演讲者鲁塞·康维尔曾经在世界各地数千次地演讲这篇演讲稿，这篇演讲稿曾经激励了美国两代人的生活信念，成功地帮助他们度过贫穷和困难，过上了富裕幸福的生活。

鲁塞·康维尔用演讲所获得的酬劳建立了一所小的神学院，用来培养帮人洗礼的神务人员，后来这所学校便发展成了现在的 Temple 大学，而且它还是工薪阶层能够上得起的大学之一。今天，它的存在就是鲁塞·康维尔为人们所留下的宝贵遗产，和他为人们所描绘的美好前景的一种见证。

这篇演讲稿由一个小故事引发而来，这个故事讲述了一位名叫阿里·哈法德的波斯人，他本来拥有大片的花园、良田和果园，可以说他是一位富人。可是自

钻石就在你身边

从有一天,当他从一位佛教僧侣的口中得知了钻石的形成过程和价值之后,他就萌生了变得更加富有的梦想,于是他就找到那位僧侣询问到哪里才可以找到钻石。

那位僧侣告诉他:"只要你能在高山之间找到一条河流,而这条河流是流淌于白沙之上的,那么你就可以在白沙中找到钻石。"

于是阿里·哈法德便卖掉了自家的农场,并收回了外借的钱财和利息,然后就出发去寻找钻石了。

可是就在他背井离乡,找遍了月亮山区和巴勒斯坦地区,以及欧洲的部分地区之后,直到他身上的钱都全部花光,却还是没能找到僧侣给他描述的河流,也没能找到钻石。在历尽沧桑之后,最后便落得衣衫褴褛、穷困潦倒,在痛苦万分的情况下,最终他纵身跳入了巴塞罗那海湾,他怀揣着被那位僧侣所激起的能得到庞大财富的诱惑,离开了这个世界。

然而,钻石究竟在哪里?阿里·哈法德背景离乡,流离失所许多年,一直苦苦寻找的钻石究竟在哪里?

热卖百年的世界级畅销书(最新译本)

几十年后的一天,阿里·哈法德的继承人竟然在牵着骆驼到花园里饮水时,在自家后院的小溪里发现了钻石,原来阿里·哈法德一直苦苦寻找的钻石就在自家后院,后来人们就在他家后院发现了人类最丰富的钻石矿——印度戈尔康达钻石矿。

阿里·哈法德生前可能曾经千万次地问过自己"钻石究竟在哪里?",原来钻石就在他家后院,可是他却为了一直就藏在自己家的财富,背井离乡,流离失所,直到后来客死他乡。虽然这个故事带有一定的调侃成分,但是,蕴含在故事中的深刻寓意却依然具有警世和震撼人心的力量。

生活在物欲横流的现代社会中,或许我们每个人都曾因在工作和生活中找不到致富的机会而郁郁寡欢,为没有致富的资本而灰心失望,为领悟不到生命的意义而悲观厌世,那么在你彷徨犹豫的时候,请读一下这篇演讲稿吧,它会告诉你许多人生的真谛。

我们的财富究竟在哪里,怎样才能更快地发现自己的价值,如何才能生活得更有意义?通过阅读这篇

钻石就在你身边

演讲稿,你全部都能找到答案。看看自己脚下的土地吧!其实,你的财富就在你的脚下,你身边的每一件事物都可能是你的"钻石矿",只要你能脚踏实地、兢兢业业地去满足人们的需求,那么你就可以拥有你想得到的一切,财富、幸福、地位和荣誉。

不要怀疑译者的推荐语,无论你从事什么行业,《钻石就在你身边》绝对有能力带给你源源不断的力量和启迪,如若不然,它如何才能获得被演讲6000多次之后,依然还这么被世界各国的人所钟爱?

鲁塞·康维尔自己的"钻石"

美国内战的第二年,也就是1862年,鲁塞·康维尔结束了他的高中生活,成功考入了耶鲁大学。可是就在他的大学生涯刚刚开始的时候,美国内战爆发了,在国家的召唤下,康维尔应征入伍成了林肯军队的一员。之后,年轻的康维尔在还不满20岁时,就被任命为陆军上校。光荣退伍之后,他就在以前陆军上校的办公室学习法律,然后获得了奥尔巴法学院的学位,成了一名真正的职业律师。

身为律师的康维尔也特别喜欢写作,他在很早的时候就开始从事写作。在1869年康维尔重返内战战场时,写了一篇反映南部战争恐怖惨状的稿子并寄给了新英格兰报社,结果这篇报道很受关注,他也因此

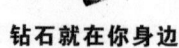
钻石就在你身边

被报社邀请成为了"波士顿夜行者"团体的成员。对他一生影响更深远的是,他成了《美国旅行者》(在波士顿出版的周刊)的通讯记者,并开始了环球旅行。

1870年,康维尔与杂志社的旅行队一起在美索不达米亚沿着底格里斯河和幼发拉底河之间的峡谷中穿行,途中在和当地的一名向导聊天的时候,康维尔听到了一些对他来说意义深远的故事。

当时的康维尔只有27岁,在他听到一则关于波斯农民阿里·哈法德的传说后,非常感动。

故事的内容是这样的:波斯农民阿里·哈法德是一位家庭富足的小农场主,一天他的佛教朋友——一位老僧侣给他讲了一个关于钻石的故事,阿里听了这个故事后很受诱惑,于是他就幻想着自己能够发现大量的钻石,成为更为富有的人。于是他就卖掉了自己肥沃的土地,开始动身去寻找巨大的钻石矿。为此他便漂泊到很远的地方。可是直到他花尽了盘缠,累得疲惫不堪还是没能找到钻石矿,最终陪伴他的只剩下衰老和穷困。在所有的梦想破灭之后,阿里·哈法德绝望地选择了投海自尽。就在他死后不久,阿里的后人竟然在自家后院的小溪里发现了不计其数的钻石。

或许在一般游客听来,这个故事不过是个迷人的传说,然而,它却唤起了康维尔心中的一个伟大信念,那就是:"人们所渴望的钻石并不一定会在偏远的山脉中,也不在遥远的海洋里。只要你能够脚踏实地地辛勤劳作,钻石就在你家后院。"

在结束这次旅行后的第二年,康维尔就开始踏实地经营起自己的事业来,而且他也因此获得了很多成绩。

康维尔在36岁的时候还在波士顿做律师,刚好当时在莱辛顿附近有一座残破不堪的教堂,人们正愁着不知道如何处置它。出于同情和乐观的心态,康维尔给当地的居民出主意,建议他们不要卖掉教堂,只要重新修葺,教堂仍可以继续被使用。居民们采纳了他的建议,并因此委任他为这座教堂的首任牧师。后来一位从费城来的执事牧师听过康维尔的讲道后,就邀请他做了费城伯克摩文大街上新建的浸信会大教

钻石就在你身边

堂的牧师。这一年是1882年,也就是从这一年开始,康维尔为当地的民众服务了43年。在这些年中,他曾多次在文苑和萧托夸社团做过激荡人心的演讲,撰写了多达40本书。此外他还为许多教堂谱写了很多圣歌,还创建了一所慈善医院……鲁塞·康维尔的人道主义精神、卓越的远见和超人的组织能力都在这些事迹中得到了充分的体现。

在1884年的一个晚上,当康维尔还在浸信会大教堂里忙活时,有个年轻人向康维尔请教了一个学术上的问题,他还表达了自己想当基督教牧师的愿望。于是康维尔很欣慰地同意了在每周挑出一个晚上的时间来教导他。让康维尔意想不到的是,到了约定的那天晚上,那位年轻人又带来了六个求知若渴的青年。这七个学生就是康维尔自己的"钻石",他的"钻石"就在他的家里、社区里,就在费城这个城市里。

有了最初的七个学生之后,前来听康维尔讲课的学生便越来越多,没过多久,这所教堂里任教的牧师也增加了一些。之后,他们开始需要租教室,后来他们又买下一两间房子。在之后的几年内,他们的学生已从七个人增加到了几百人。1888年,他们组建了Temple大学,并获得了设立许可,康维尔理所当然地被推选为校长,而且他的任期长达三十八年之久。

让康维尔一举成名于天下知的演讲就可以说是他的著名演讲稿《钻石就在你身边》,这个演讲稿使康维尔成为了美国顶尖的演说家。他曾在自己生活的那片土地上的很多地方多次地发表这篇演说,直到1925年,也就是他生命的最后一年,他一共将这个演讲稿演说了6000多次,在当时的美国有成千上万的民众曾在教堂、公共讲台,或者收音机旁边听过他的这个演讲,直到今天,他那篇既实用又充满乐观精神的文章仍然在被世界各地的人们翻阅。

就在康维尔演讲《钻石就在你身边》达到5000次的时候,费城音乐学院将一把金钥匙授予给了他,以表示宾州人民对他的感激之情。

在美国以他的名字命名的公立学校有两所,一所位于康维尔的居住地——麻州华盛顿区,另一所位于

钻石就在你身边

费城。

其中在费城校区行政大楼的东侧顶端,有一尊康维尔的半身雕像,而且位于哈里斯郡的宾州教育总部大楼的墙壁上也刻有康维尔的名字,就连 Temple 大学的一座礼堂也是以康维尔的名字命名的。在 1922 年,康维尔还获得了万内斯会社颁给他的"卓越贡献奖"。不过,康维尔所获得的最高荣誉却是在 1923 获得的宾州奖,这个奖项在每年都只发给为当地贡献最大的公民。

鲁塞·康维尔去世之后被葬在了创建者花园,整个花园四周被 Temple 大学雄伟的建筑所环绕,康维尔就长眠于其中。整个 Temple 大学本身就是康维尔永久的纪念碑,是他永远的"钻石之地"。

热卖百年的世界级畅销书（最新译本）

前 言
Preface

我很惊讶，这篇演讲稿能够被这么多人一遍又一遍地聆听、阅读，而且它已经成了心理学的一个研究对象；虽然这篇演讲稿有悖于一切正统演讲稿的规则，又突破了修辞的限制，但它仍然是我在57年的公众生活中最受欢迎的演讲稿。

在众多的演讲稿中，有时为了一篇演讲稿，我要花费一年多的时间来精心地调查研究，而且我的演讲稿，我通常都只演讲一次，我从不演讲重复的内容。而且我通常都会为我的演讲稿花费很多的心血，可是《钻石就在你身边》却是个例外，我没有为它花费太多的心血，只不过是随意地把资料拼凑了在一起，然后就放手去演讲，甚至可以说我都没有为它做什么特别的准备，但是

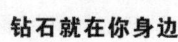
钻石就在你身边

它却取得了成功,而我一再研究,不断调整计划的事物却是一种完全的失败。

经历了这么多年以后,在这座城市里很多"藏在各家后院的钻石"已经被人们发现,你也可以发现"你家后院的钻石"。因为,很多人都已经发现了,要知道只要人们去做了,就一定能做成一件事。虽然这些故事很多都能在附近任何一家图书馆里找到,但是除了用这些我已经一再讲述过的故事来论证我的理论之外,我想不出还有什么别的更好的方法了。

——鲁塞·康维尔

热卖百年的世界级畅销书(最新译本)

前　言
Preface

I am astonished that so many people should care to hear this story over and over again. Indeed, this lecture has become a study in psychology; it often breaks all rules of oratory, departs from the precepts of rhetoric, and yet remains the most popular of any lecture I have delivered in the fifty-seven years of my public life. I have sometimes studied for a year upon a lecture and made careful research, and then presented the lecture just once—never delivered it again. I put too much work on it. But this had no work on it—thrown together perfectly at random, spoken off hand without any special preparation, and it succeeds when the thing we study, work over, adjust to a plan, is an

钻石就在你身边

entire failure.

The "Acres of Diamonds" which I have mentioned through so many years are to be found in this city, and you are to find them. Many people have found them. And what man has done, man can do. I could not find anything better to illustrate my thought than a story I have told over and over again, and which is now found in books in nearly every library.

——Russell H. Conwell

热卖百年的世界级畅销书(最新译本)

目 录
contents

哪里可以找到钻石 / 1

Where to find your diamonds?

钻石就在你家后院 / 21

Diamonds are in your acres

你没有权利做一个穷人 / 41

You have no right to be poor

人们对你的评判正是你成功的见证 / 54

You can judge your success in others' words about you

常识才是你致富最需要的资本 / 62

Common sense is the capital for you to be rich

满足了人们的需求你就能致富 / 72

You will be rich when you know what people need

你无法致富是因为你感到沮丧 / 84

You can't get rich because you feel depressed

伟大的恰好就是简单的 / 94

The greatest just is the simplest

你的财富就在你身边 / 104

Your wealth is just on your side

你也能成为伟人 / 123

You also can be a great man

后记:我的故事 / 156

Postscipt: My Story

热卖百年的世界级畅销书(最新译本)

哪里可以找到钻石
Where to find your diamonds?

1870年,我们在巴格达雇了一名向导,顺着底格里斯河一路游览。他带领我们从波西波里斯开始,沿途游历了尼尼微、巴比伦,直到阿拉伯湾的亚述古帝国遗址。我们的这位向导先生对这一带的人文风景可以说是了如指掌,而且他对游客还十分的热情。他就像理发师在帮人理发时会不断讲故事给你听,从而使你不会去在意他在你头上又抓又挠。他就是这样,一连串跟我讲了好多故事,以至于我都已经不胜其烦了,直到后来我只好拒绝听他讲,只要他一开口讲话,我就把脸转向别处，我想我的这一举动肯定让他颇为恼火。

我还记得那天将近傍晚时，他突然摘下头上的土耳其小帽，然后用手不停地在空中挥舞。我对他的这一举动非常不解，可是我又不愿意去多看他一眼，真担心一看又被他抓住没完没了地讲故事给我听。可是，我又是一个很好奇的人，最后还是忍不住朝他看了过去。很快，我好奇的目光被他逮了个正着，这个向导我们雇得可真是划得来，他又可以开始喋喋不休了。这次他很神秘地对我说道："我现在要再给你讲一个故事，这个故事我从来都只讲给最好的朋友听！"既然他都把话说到这份儿上了，我也只好尽一点好朋友的义务，听他讲这个故事吧。于是我就听了他接下来讲的故事，直到现在，我还一直都在庆幸自己当初听了他讲的这个故事。他讲道：

从前有一个名叫阿里·哈法德的波斯人，住在离印度河不远的地方。他拥有一大片农场,那里有果园、田地和花园。他是个知足而且富有的人——或许因为他富有,所以他才会很知足;还可能是因为他知足,所以他才很富有。有一天,一位老僧侣来拜访阿里·哈法德,被请进屋后,老僧侣就坐在阿里·哈法德身边的火炉旁跟他讲述了人类世界形成的过程。

他说,人们生存的这个世界最初只是一团雾气,后来,上帝把自己的手指伸入了雾中,然后缓缓转动手指搅动雾气,而且逐渐加快速度,最后终于把那团雾旋转成一个固体大火球,之后这个火球就在宇宙中滚动,穿过其他宇宙迷雾不停地燃烧前进,直到它失去水汽,这时上帝便开始降下倾盆大雨,冷却了滚热的地表外壳。然后火球内部的火焰冲出冷却的地壳,形成了我们美好地球上的高山和河谷。就在内部熔岩涌出地壳时,迅速冷却的物质,就形成了花岗石;冷却稍慢一点的就变成了白银;再慢一点的,就变成了黄金;最后冷却的物质才凝结成了钻石。老僧侣接着说道:"钻石就是由阳光凝结而成的物质。"

从科学上来讲,他这么说是正确的,因为大家都知道钻石其实就是一种纯炭物质,可以折射阳光。接着,那位老僧侣又讲了一个故事,这个故事我永远都不会忘记。他讲道:

钻石是上帝最后创造的矿物质,是矿物中最高级的物质;女人是上帝最后创造的动物,是动物中最高级的。我认为,这就是为什么钻石与女人总是如此相得益彰的原因。

之后老僧侣又告诉阿里·哈法德说,如果他能拥有一大捧钻石,就可以把整个国家的土地都买下;如果他要是拥有一座钻石矿场,就可以利用这笔巨额财富,成功地把他的孩子扶上王位。

阿里·哈法德听了这些有关钻石的故事,知道了钻石价值的之后,那天晚上在他入睡之前，他就已经把自己当成了一个穷人——不是因为他失去了什么东西，而是他开始变得不满足，所以才会觉得自己很穷；也是因为他认为自己很穷，所以才会变得不满足。他不停地想："我要是有一座钻石矿该多好呀。"因此，他一整夜都没能入睡，第二天一大早，他就跑去找那位僧侣。

以我的经验来看，那位老僧侣一大早被吵醒肯定很不高兴。可是哈法德却没意识到这一点，他迫不及待地把老僧侣从睡梦中摇醒，然后问他说："你能告诉我在什么地方可以找到钻石吗？"

"找钻石？你要钻石做什么？"老僧侣不解地问道。

"我想要变得富有无比，"阿里·哈法德说，"可是我却不知道到哪里才可以找到钻石"。

"哦，"老僧侣这才明白了阿里·哈法德的

钻石就在你身边

心思。于是他就说,"这个简单,只要你在山间找到一条从白沙上流过的河流,就可以在沙子里找到钻石了"。

"可是,你真的认为会有这样的河流吗?"

"这样的河流很多,很多,只要你去找,就一定能找到。"

"那好吧,我这就去找。"阿里·哈法德说。

从老僧侣那里回去之后,阿里·哈法德就卖掉了他的农场,收回了所有的借款,把自家的房子和家人交给邻居照看和照顾,之后他就出发去寻找钻石了。

在我看来,他最初寻找钻石的方向很正确。他先去了月亮山区,之后又去了巴勒斯坦地区,后来又去了欧洲,直到最后他花光了身上所有的钱,变得穷困潦倒、衣衫褴褛、身上又脏又臭。当站在西班牙巴塞罗那海湾边时,他看到一道道巨浪越过赫拉克勒斯石柱涌来,此时,这位饱经风霜、痛不欲生的穷人再也忍受不了折磨，最后纵身一跳，就被卷入了翻滚不息的浪涛里，再也没能回头看一眼，就离开了这个世界。

讲述完这个悲伤的故事，我们的向导停了下来，他拉住我骑的骆驼的缰绳，然后转身去扶正另一头骆驼背上的行李。我记得当时听完这个故事，我心中充满了疑惑："向导先生为什么只把这个故事讲给他最好的朋友听呢？"这个故事好像并没有什么特别的地方，好像没有开头，没有过程，也没有结尾——好像什么都没有。以前，我从来没有听过或看过这样的故事，这是我所听的故事中，第一个刚开始主角就死了的故事。我只听了这个故事的一个章节，而且在这个章节里，主角就死了。

不一会儿，我们的向导就又走了回来，然后牵着我骑的骆驼的缰绳继续往前走，我们的故事也跟着继续，他接着讲道：

钻石就在你身边

有一天,阿里·哈法德的后人带骆驼去花园的小溪边喝水,当骆驼刚把鼻子伸到花园那清澈见底的溪水中时,阿里·哈法德的后人突然发现,这条浅浅的溪底白沙中闪烁着奇异的光芒。于是他就伸下手去,捞起一块黑石头,这块石头上面有一小处闪亮的地方,这个亮点居然能从阳光里折射出彩虹般的色彩。于是他就把这块怪异的鹅卵石拿进了屋里,放在了壁炉台子上,之后就继续忙他的工作去了,后来他也就把这件事给忘得一干二净了。

几天之后,那位曾经告诉阿里·哈法德钻石是如何形成的僧侣前来拜访他的后人。当他看到壁炉台子上那块闪闪发光的鹅卵石的时候,他立即凑上前去,然后惊喜地叫道:"这是一块钻石!这是一块钻石!难道是阿里·哈法德回来了吗?"

"不,不,阿里·哈法德还没回来,那也不

热卖百年的世界级畅销书（最新译本）

是什么钻石，它不过是一块普通的鹅卵石，是我在自家后院发现的。"

"真的吗？我只要看一眼就知道它是不是钻石，"僧侣很确定地强调说，"这真的是钻石！"

之后，他们就一起奔向后院的小溪边，当他们用手捧起溪底的白沙时，又发现了许多比第一颗更璀璨、更值钱的钻石。

接着，向导就对我说，这就是人们发现印度戈尔康达（GOL-conda）钻石矿的全过程。它的价值远远超过南非的金伯利（Kimberley）钻石矿，这个钻石矿是有史以来人类发现的最大的钻石矿。英王皇冠上的库伊努尔大钻石（Kohinoor，106克拉），以及我一直希望俄国能够为了日俄和平而出售给日本的那颗镶嵌在俄王王冠上的世界上最大的钻石，都采自于那座钻石矿。

后来直到向导再次从头上取下他那顶土耳其小帽，然后拿在手里在空中挥舞，示意我

钻石就在你身边

记住这个故事所能带给人们的启示时，我才从这个故事的情节当中回过神来。

虽然那个向导讲的故事并非个个都很有意义，但是他所讲的每一个故事都带有深刻的寓意。最后他说，假如阿里·哈法德留在了家乡，勤恳地翻种自家的田地、打理自家的花园，他就不会沦落到流离失所、挨饿受穷、贫困潦倒的地步，更不会跳海而死。那样他就会发现他所拥有的是一块多么神奇的土地，在那里他可以拥有"遍地的钻石"，没错，是遍地的钻石，每一寸土地都是钻石。后来证明在他那块古老的农场里每挖出一锄的泥土中，都能找到无数颗能够装饰王冠的钻石。

热卖百年的世界级畅销书(最新译本)

哪里可以找到钻石
Where to find your diamonds?

In 1870 we went down the Tigris River. We hired a guide at Baghdad to show us Persepolis, Nineveh and Babylon, and the ancient countries of Assyria as far as the Arabian Gulf. He was well acquainted with the land, but he was one of those guides who love to entertain their patrons; he was like a barber that tells you many stories in order to keep your mind off the scratching and the scraping. He told me so many stories that I grew tired of his telling them and I refused to listen— looked away whenever he commenced, that made

钻石就在你身边

the guide quite angry.

I remember that toward evening he took his Turkish cap off his head and swang it around in the air. The gesture I did not understand and I did not dare look at him for fear I should become the victim of another story. But, although I am not a woman, I did look, and the instant I turned my eyes upon that worthy guide he was off again. Said he, "I will tell you a story now which I reserve for my particular friends!" So then, counting myself as a particular friend, I listened, and I have always been glad I did.

He said:there once lived not far from the River Indus and ancient Persian by the name of Al Hafed. He said that Al Hafed owned a very large farm with orchards, grain fields and gardens. He was a contented and wealthy man—contented because he was wealthy, and wealthy because he

热卖百年的世界级畅销书(最新译本)

was contented. One day there visited this old farmer one of those ancient Buddhist priests, and he sat down by Al Hafed's fire and told that old farmer how this world of ours was made.

He said that this world was once a mere bank of fog, which is scientifically true, and he said that the Almighty thrust his finger into the bank of fog, and then began slowly to move his finger around and gradually to increase the speed of his finger until at last he whirled that bank of fog into a solid ball of fire, and it went rolling through the universe, burning its way through other cosmic banks of fog, until it condensed the moisture without, and fell in floods of rain upon the heated surface and cooled the outward crust. Then the internal flames burst through the cooling crust and threw up the mountains and made the hills and the valleys of this wonderful world of ours. If this internal melted mass burst out and cooled very quickly it became granite; that which cooled less quickly became silver; and less quickly, gold; and after gold diamonds were made. Said the old priest, "A diamond is a congealed drop of sunlight."

This is a scientific truth also. You all know that a diamond is pure carbon, actually deposited sunlight—and he said another thing I would not forget: he declared that a diamond is the last and highest of God's mineral creations, as a woman is the last and highest of God's animal creations. I suppose that is the reason why the two have such a liking for each other. And the old priest told Al Hafed that if he had a handful of diamonds he could purchase a whole country, and with a mine of diamonds he could place his children upon thrones through the influence of their great wealth.

Al Hafed heard all about diamonds and how much they were worth, and went to his bed that night a poor man—not that he had lost anything, but poor because he was discontented and discontented because he thought he was poor. He said: "I want a mine of diamonds!" So he lay awake all night, and early in the morning sought out the priest.

Now I know from experience that a priest when awakened early in the morning is cross. He awoke that priest out of his dreams and said to him: "Will you tell me where I can find diamonds?"

The priest said: "Diamonds? What do you want with diamonds?"

"I want to be immensely rich," said Al Hafed, "but I don't know where to find."

钻石就在你身边

"Well," said the priest, "if you will find river that runs over white sand between high mountains, in those sands you will always see diamonds."

"Do you really believe that there is such a river?"

"Plenty of them, plenty of them, all you have to do is just go and find them, then you have them." Al Hafed said, "I will go."

So he sold his farm, collected his money at interest, left his family in charge of a neighbor, and away he went in search of diamonds. He began very properly, to my mind, at the Mountains of the Moon. Afterwards he went around into Palestine, then wandered on into Europe, and at last, when his money was all spent, and he was in rags, wretchedness and poverty, he stood on the shore of that bay in Barcelona, Spain, when a

热卖百年的世界级畅销书(最新译本)

tidal wave came rolling in through the Pillars of Hercules and the poor, afflicted, suffering man could not resist the awful temptation to cast himself into that incoming tide, and he sank beneath its foaming crest, never to rise in this life again.

When that old guide had told me that very sad story, he stopped the camel I was riding and went back to fix the baggage on one of the other camels, and I remember thinking to myself, "Why did he reserve that for his particular friends? " There seemed to be no beginning, middle or end—nothing to it. That was the first story I ever heard or read in which the hero was killed in the first chapter. I had but one chapter of that story and the hero was dead. When the guide came back and took up the halter of my camel again, he went right on with the same story. He said that Al Hafed's successor led his camel

钻石就在你身边

out into the garden to drink, and as that camel put its nose down into the clear water of the garden brook, Al Hafed's successor noticed a curious flash of light from the sands of the shallow stream, and reaching in he pulled out a black stone having an eye of light that reflected all the colors of the rainbow, and he took that curious pebble into the house and left it on the mantel, then went on his way and forgot all about it.

A few days after that, this same old priest who told Al Hafed how diamonds were made, came in to visit his successor, when he saw that flash of light from the mantel. He rushed up and said: "Here is a diamond—here is a diamond! Has Al Hafed returned?" " No, no, Al Hafed has not returned and that is not a diamond, that is nothing but a stone, we found it right out here in our garden." "But I know a diamond when I see it." Said he: "that is a diamond!"

Then together they rushed to the garden and stirred up the white sands with their fingers and found others more beautiful, more valuable diamonds than the first, and thus, said the guide to me, were discovered the diamond mines of Golconda, the most magnificent diamond mines in all the history of mankind, exceeding the Kimberley in its value. The great Kohinoor diamond in England's crown jewels and the largest crown diamond on earth in Russia's crown jewels, which I had often hoped she would have to sell before they had peace with Japan, came from that mine, and when the old guide had called my attention to that wonderful discovery, he took his Turkish cap off his head again and swung it around in the air to call my attention to the moral.

Those Arab guides have a moral to each sto-

钻石就在你身边

ry, though the stories are not always moral. He said had Al Hafed remained at home and dug in his own cellar or in his own garden, instead of wretchedness, starvation, poverty and death—a strange land, he would have had "acres of diamonds"—for every acre, yes, every shovelful of that old farm afterwards revealed the gems which since have decorated the crowns of monarchs.

热卖百年的世界级畅销书（最新译本）

钻石就在你家后院
Diamonds are in your acres

听完向导激情飞扬地谈论这个故事所蕴含的道理后，我才终于明白这位向导为什么要把这个故事保留起来，只讲给自己最好的朋友听。不过，我并没有把自己的这一发现告诉那位老向导，而且我也并不打算告诉他。因为那位老向导不过是在告诉我，像我这样在底格里斯河游览的美国青年，最好待在自己的美国老家，不要到处跑。只不过他的处世态度更像个律师，更趋向于用委婉的方式来表达他不敢直言的事情。最后，我还是没有告诉

钻石就在你身边

他，其实我已经明白了他所要表达的意思。

之后，我告诉他，他的故事使我想起了另一个故事，然后我就把这个故事讲给他听了。

1847年，有一个人在美国的加利福尼亚州拥有一座农场。一天，他从报纸上得知，人们在加州南部发现了金矿。于是，他就把自己的农场卖给了苏特上校，之后就动身去加州南部淘金了。苏特上校买了农场之后，就在农场后面的小溪边盖了一座小磨坊。一天，苏特上校的小女儿从磨坊的水沟里挖了一些潮湿的沙子，想带回屋里玩，可是沙子太湿了，于是她就准备把沙子洒在壁炉前烘干。就在她用手捧起沙子的时候，一位来访的客人恰好在沙子流出她指缝的时候发现了一些闪闪发光的沙粒，这种沙粒和在加州最早发现的黄金一样。可是那个一心想要寻找黄金的加州佬却早已把他的这座农场卖掉而背井离乡了，之后，他再也没有回来过。

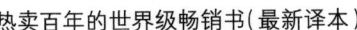
热卖百年的世界级畅销书(最新译本)

两年前,我在加州发表这篇演讲时,当时的演讲地点刚好就在距离那座农场不远的地方。那儿的人们告诉我,那座金矿在当时还在开采,拥有农场三分之一股份的主人,近几年来无论是醒着还是在睡觉,平均每十五分钟都能从这座矿场里获得价值二十美元的黄金。

天啊,但愿有一天,你我都能有这样的机会,能够拥有这样的收入。事实上我所知道的能够说明这个道理的例子还有很多,其中最好的一个例子就发生在宾夕法尼亚州。

之前,有个人在当地拥有一座农场,可是他却把它卖掉了。不过,如果我在宾州也有一座农场,说不定我也会像他那样把农场卖掉。他在卖掉农场之前,先是找了一份工作:去加拿大替他表哥经营收售煤油的生意。因为在加拿大先发现了煤油,所以这个农场主才决定去找加拿大的表哥谋一份差事。由此看来，这位农场主并不傻——在尚未找到其他工作之前，他还是愿意继续留在自己的农场里的。

然而事实上，在各种各样的傻子中，最傻的人就莫过于在还没有找到新工作之前，就辞掉了原来的工作。这句话要用在我的同行们身上就再合适不过了，不过对于想要离婚的人可就不能套用这句话了。所以我说那位农场主在没有找到其他的活计之前是不会离开他的农场的。可是，当那位农场主写信给加拿大的表哥后，他表哥却回信说不能雇用他，因为他对石油生意一窍不通。农场主只好回信说："没关系，我会去好好学习相关知识的。"之后，他就开始下定决心学习有关石油方面的全部知识。从第二天起他就开始潜心学习，从最简单的物质特性，一直研究到煤油炼出，他几乎了解了这一行业的所有知识。然后，他又写信给他的表哥说："现在，我对煤油方面的业务已经很了解了。"于是他表哥回信给他:"那就太好了,你过来吧。"

根据当地资料记载,这个农场主将他的农场以833美元一分不多的价格卖给了别人。

几乎就在他刚刚离开农场后,新的农场主就开始着手处理牛的饮水问题,他发现,农场的前主人已把这件事处理得很妥当了。在这座农场里,有一条小溪从附近的山坡上流下来,之前的农场主就拿一块厚木板以一定的角度横放在小溪上,从而将小溪的水流面变宽,将一边的水面比另一面压低几英寸,将水面上的泡沫挡在另一边。前主人之所以用这种方式摆放木板,主要是为了防止农场的牛看到吓人的泡沫后不敢到溪里喝水,而摆放了木板之后,牛儿就可以从溪流没有泡沫的一边喝水了。

虽然前任农场主的木板放置得很巧妙,可是他却挡住了已经连续流了23年之久的

钻石就在你身边

石油。他哪里知道那些可怕的泡沫就是石油！据宾夕法尼亚州的官方报道,地质学家早在1870年就估算出,这口井将为该州赚进1亿美元。现在,在那座农场的原址上,已经建立了泰特斯维尔市,那口名为普莱森特尔的油井仍然在冒油。我不得不再次重申,那位原来几乎已经学习了石油形成的所有知识的农场主人,却在他想要到加拿大赚钱的第二天便把这座农场以833美元一分不多的价格卖给了别人。而这笔钱和他的农场所能带给他的财富相比,简直不值得一提。

讲到此,我又想起了用另外一个故事来论证这个论点,故事发生在马萨诸塞州,很不好意思,因为那里刚好是我的老家。

故事的主人公生于马萨诸塞州,后来他离开那里去耶鲁大学,学习矿物知识。到大四的时候,学校以周薪15美元,请他在课余时间帮那些成绩差的学生指导课程,他接受了这份差事，靠这些薪水供自己读完了大学。毕业后，学校将他的周薪从15美元上调到45美元，聘请他担任教授，可是他却没有接受。相反他直接回到了老家，对他的母亲说："妈妈，我不想做每周只有45美元的工作，我认为像我这种头脑的人，怎么可以每周只拿到45美元的薪水呢?! 妈妈，我们到加州去吧，在那里只要我们能淘到黄金，我们就能马上变成富翁！"母亲回答他说："还是不要去的好，要知道平静而快乐的生活和发财是一样可贵。"

可是，他是家里的独生子，母亲最后还是让步了——他们家向来如此。他们卖掉了老家的财产，搬到威斯康星州。之后，这位青年人开始在一家铜矿业公司就职，他的薪水仍然是从15美元一周开始，如果他为公司发现了金矿，就可以分得红利。

虽然我从来没有听说过他发现了什么金

钻石就在你身边

矿,不过,我却听说了一些后来发生在他老家的事情。他们离开老家后不久,买下他们房子的农夫出去挖马铃薯时,想把马铃薯装在大篮子里从前门带进屋里,可是门口两旁的石墙靠得太近了,以至于夹住了大篮子。于是,那位农夫就把篮子放在了地上,想把篮子拉进屋里,他先往一边拉了一下,毫无起色,然后他又往另一边一拉,结果篮子被紧紧地夹在门口。顺便说一下,我们麻州的农场的大门大多是用石头砌的。最后,农夫只好竭尽力气使劲把篮子往里拉,就在这时他突然注意到,门槛上层的一个台阶上的一块石头很特别,在这块石头上嵌着一大块天然白银!而那位不愿屈就于每周45美元的薪水的矿物学教授可能在出售麻州老家这幢住宅时,就坐在那块石头上和买主讨价还价。他从小就在这栋房子里长大,一直在那块白银旁边跑来跑去,可能他的衣袖和裤管也曾在那块白银上面磨擦过，而这块石头也好像在说："快过来呀，过来呀，快呀，我可是一块价值几十万美元的白银，你怎么不把我挖走呢？"

可是那名青年人却永远都不可能再有机会把它挖走了。纽伯瑞港没有白银，哪里才有白银？我不知道，可能其他地方会有，可是后来他也没有挖到什么，亏他还是个矿物学教授呢！

我想再也没有比整晚都在这里讲述那个教授所犯的错更有趣的事了，可是我却很想知道目前那个教授在威斯康星做什么。我可以想象他坐在壁炉前面，对他的朋友说："你们认不认识一个住在费城名叫康维尔的人？"

"哦，是的，我听说过他。"

"那你们是否也认得和他住在同一个城市的琼斯？"

"认得呀，我知道有这么个人。"

之后，他就会开始笑个不停，还会一边

钻石就在你身边

笑,一边对他的朋友说:"他们和我犯过同样的错误,完全一样的错误。"这句话并非只是个笑话,因为你我也都犯过同样的错。

热卖百年的世界级畅销书(最新译本)

钻石就在你家后院
Diamonds are in your acres

When he had given the moral to his story, I saw why he had reserved this story for his "particular friends." I didn't tell him I could see it; and I was not going to tell that old guide that I could see it. For it was that mean old guide's way of going around such a thing, like a lawyer, and saying indirectly what he did not dare say directly, that there was a certain young man that day traveling down the Tigris River that might better be at home in America. I didn't tell him I could

钻石就在你身边

see it.

I told him his story reminded me of one, and I told it to him quick. I told him about that man out in California, who, in 1847, owned a ranch out there. He read that gold had been discovered in Southern California, and then he sold his ranch to Colonel Sutter and started off to hunt for gold. Colonel Sutter put a mill on the little stream in that farm, and one day his little girl brought some wet sand from the raceway of the mill into the house and placed it before the fire to dry, and as that sand was falling through the little girl's fingers a visitor saw the first shining scales of real gold that were ever discovered in California. But the man who wanted the gold had sold his ranch and gone away, never to return.

I delivered this lecture two years ago in California, in the city that stands near that farm, and they told me that the mine is not exhausted yet, and that a one-third owner of that farm has been getting during these recent years twenty dollars of gold every fifteen minutes of his life, sleeping or waking. Why you and I would enjoy an income like that!

But the best illustration that I have know of this thought was found here in Pennsylvania. There was a man living in Pennsylvania who owned a farm here and he did what I should do if I had a farm in Pennsylvania—he sold it. But before he sold it he concluded to secure employment collecting coal oil for his cousin in Canada. They first discovered coal oil there, so this farmer in Pennsylvania decided that he would apply for a position with his cousin in Canada. Now you see, the farmer was not altogether a foolish man. He did not leave his farm until he had something else

钻石就在你身边

to do.

Of all the simpletons the stars shine on there is none more foolish than a man who leaves one job before he has obtained another. And that has especial reference to gentlemen of my profession, and has no reference to a man seeking a divorce. So I say this old farmer did not leave one job until he had obtained another. He wrote to Canada. But his cousin replied that he could not engage him because he did not know anything about the oil business. "Well, then," said he, "I will understand it." So he set himself at the study of the whole subject. He began at the second day of the creation, he studied the subject from the primitive vegetation to the coal oil stage, until he know all about it. Then he wrote to his cousin and said: "Now I understand the oil business." And his cousin replied to him: "All right, then, come on."

热卖百年的世界级畅销书（最新译本）

That man, by the record of the country, sold his farm for eight hundred and thirty-three dollars—even money, "no cents." He had scarcely gone from that farm before the man who purchased it went out to arrange for watering the cattle and he found that the previous owner had arranged the matter very nicely. There is a stream running down the hillside there, and the previous owner had gone out and put a plank across that stream at an angle, exceeding across the brook and down edgewise a few inches under the surface of the water. The purpose of the plank across that brook was to throw over to the other bank a dreadful-looking scum through which the cattle would not put their noses to drink above the plank, although they would drink the water on one side below it.

Thus that man who had gone to Canada had

钻石就在你身边

been himself damming back for twenty-three years a flow of coal oil which the State Geologist of Pennsylvania declared officially, as early as 1870, was then worth to our state a hundred millions of dollars. The city of Titusville now stands on that farm and those Pleasantville wells flow on, and that farmer who had studied all about the formation of oil since the second day of God's creation clear down to the present time, sold that farm for $833, no cents—again I say, "no sense." But I need another illustration, and I found that in Massachusetts, and I am sorry I did, because that is my old state. This young man I mentioned went out of the state to study—went down to Yale College and studied mines and mining. They paid him fifteen dollars a week during his last year for training students who were behind their classes in mineralogy. Out of hours, of course, while pursu-

热卖百年的世界级畅销书(最新译本)

ing his own studies. But when he graduated, they raised his pay from fifteen dollars to forty-five dollars and offered him a professorship. Then he went straight home to his mother and said: "mother, I won't work for forty-five dollars a week. What is forty-five dollars a week for a man with a brain like mine! Mother, let's go out to California and stake out gold claims and be immensely rich." "no," said his mother, "it is just as well to be happy as it is to be rich." But as he was the only son in his family—they always do; and they sold homestead out in Massachusetts and went to Wisconsin, where he went into the employ of the Superior Copper Mining Company, and he was start from sight in the employ of that company at fifteen dollars a week again. He was also to have an interest in any mines that he should discover for that company. But I do not believe that

钻石就在你身边

he has ever discovered a mine—I do not know anything about it, but I do not believe he has. I know he had scarcely gone from the old homestead before the farmer who had bought the homestead went out to dig potatoes, and he was bringing them in a large basket through the front gateway, the ends of the stone wall came so near together at the gate that the basket hugged very tight. So he set the basket on the ground and pulled, first on one side and then on the other side. Our farms in Massachusetts are mostly stone walls, and the farmers have to be economical with their gateways in order to have some places to put the stones. That basket hugged so tight there that as he was hauling it through he noticed in the upper stone next the gate a block of native silver, eight inches square; and this professor of mines, mining and mineralogy, who would not work for forty-five dollars a week, when he sold that homestead in Massachusetts, sat right on that stone to make the bargain. He was brought up there; he had gone back and forth by that piece of silver, rubbed it with his sleeve, and it seemed to say: "Come now, now, quick, here is a hundred thousand dollars. Why not take me?" But he would not take it. There was no silver in Newburyport; it was all away off—well, I don't know where; he didn't, but somewhere else—and he was a professor of mineralogy.

I do not know of anything I would enjoy better than to take the whole time tonight telling of blunders like that I have heard professors made. Yet I wish I knew what that man is doing out there in Wisconsin. I can imagine him out there, as he sits by his fireside, saying to his friends:

"Do you know that man Conwell that lives in

钻石就在你身边

Philadelphia?"

"Oh, yes, I have heard of him."

"And do you know that man Jones that lives in the same city of him?"

"Yes, I have heard of him."

And then he begins to laugh and laugh and says to his friends, "They have done the same thing I did, precisely." And that spoils the whole joke, because you and I have done it.

热卖百年的世界级畅销书(最新译本)

你没有权利做一个穷人
You have no right to be poor

今晚在座的人当中大概有百分之九十的人今天都在犯着同样的错误。在我看来,你们都应该是富翁,你们没有权利成为一名穷人。生活在费城而不富有,这真是一种不幸,而且是双重不幸。因为你本来就应该可以像沦为穷人一样成为富人。费城有这么多致富的机会,你们都应该成为富人。听到这些话,那些持有偏见的人可能会质问我:"你怎么可以毫不吝惜自己的时间去劝告正在成长的一代人把时间都花费在挣钱上?一分钱、一块钱地去挣,你这种说教参杂了太多商业化的观念!"

可是,我必须告诉你们,你们真的应该花费时间使自己富裕起来。我们大家都知道,世上确实是有些东西比金钱更有价值,而且对这一点,我们也深信不疑。可是,当我看到一座萧条凄凉的坟墓时,我们便会由衷地产生一种难以名状的悲伤,那时,我就能更深地体会到有些东西是比金钱更重要、更崇高、更值得追求。或许那些曾经经历过苦难的人才会更深地体会到,有某些东西比黄金更甜蜜、更神圣、更威严。可是,所有的这一切在普通人的意识里全都要靠金钱来实现和提升。金钱就是力量!

爱情是世界上帝所创造的最崇高的事物,可是只有拥有大量金钱的情人,才能使得他的爱情更加甜蜜。金钱就是力量!金钱就具有这样的力量。如果有人说:"我不想要金钱",那他就无异于在说:"我不想为我的同胞们带来任何帮助和利益。"这么说很显然是荒谬的,可是如果要把两者分开,也同样是荒谬的。我们的生命原本是精彩而伟大的,你们真的应该花点儿时间去赚钱,因为金钱蕴含着无穷的力量。或许,听到我的这些话,某些持有强烈的宗教偏见的人会有不同的看法,他们中有些人认为,能够成为一名上帝的贫穷子民,是一种荣耀。可能现在在我眼前就有一些人持有这种想法。

曾经在一个祈祷会上,我听见一个人在做祷告,他很感激上帝,让他成为他的一名贫穷子民。听到他的祷告,我不禁心想,这话要是被他的妻子听到,她会作何感想?因为贫穷,她不得不靠替别人洗东西来维持他们的生活,而她的丈夫却悠闲地坐在走廊里抽烟。我真是再也不愿看到这样的上帝的贫穷子民了。正是因为某些人有这种想法,所以一些原本应该很富有的人,现在却变得贫穷、懦弱,这些人都犯了一个极为严重的错误。他们不仅没有做到忠于自己，还连累了自己的同胞。事实上，只要我们采用基督徒的方式和手段去挣钱，我们很快就能致富，而且这正是我们能够迅速致富的唯一方法。

我记得几年以前，有位年轻的神学院学生来到我办公室，对我说，他认为有义务也必须来和我"谈谈"，因为他看到经书上说，金钱是万恶之源。我问他是哪本经书上这么说的，他说是《圣经》上这么说的。我问他，他是否自创了一本新的《圣经》。他说没有，他并没有得到新的《圣经》，他是在原来的《圣经》上读到的。"那么，"我说，"就算这句话在我的《圣经》上也有，可我却从来没有看到过。能否麻烦你拿本《圣经》来，让我见识一下这句话到底在哪儿？"

他离开房间，不一会儿便趾高气昂地走了回来，手上捧着一本摊开的《圣经》，还表现出一种心胸狭窄的教士所特有的偏执和骄傲的神情，自以为在误解《圣经》的人面前发现了至理名言。他把《圣经》放在我面前的桌子上，然后阴阳怪气地对我说道："就在这儿，你可以自己读一下。"我对他说："年轻人，等你年纪稍大一点后，你就会明白，你是不能听信和你观点不同的人替你念《圣经》的。"我说。"你看，你对《圣经》有不同的理解，所以请你替我念一段《圣经》，同时你要记着，学校教你的是更要看重人们对《圣经》的理解。"于是他就拿起《圣经》念道："热衷金钱，是万恶之源。"他读的没错。

的确，《圣经》可以使人想起人类的尊严与关爱，是她带给了人类最伟大的智慧。所以，你可以引用这上面的话，并将你的生死都托付于她，而无须带着任何恐慌。因此，他在引用《圣经》时，其实是在引用真理。"热衷金钱，是万恶之源。"的确如此，只不过热衷金

钻石就在你身边

钱不过是一种手段,而不是目的。毋庸置疑,如果没有手段,你就达不到目标。如果一个人崇拜金钱,而不信仰利用金钱能够达到的目的,那么,他就成了一个名副其实的守财奴,对他来说金钱真的就是万恶之源了。想想看,如果你没有钱,你能为你的妻子、孩子,以及你的家庭和你所生活的城市做些什么事情呢?再想想看,如果你没有钱,你怎么可能随心所欲地捐钱给Temple学院作基金呢?可是现在,朋友们,却有人指责你不该把时间放在赚钱上,这是多么的前后矛盾呀!所以,我们应该富有,有了金钱我们就能做很多事情。

热卖百年的世界级畅销书(最新译本)

你没有权利做一个穷人
You have no right to be poor

Ninety out of every hundred people here have made that mistake this very day. I say you ought to be rich; you have no right to be poor. To live in Philadelphia and not be rich is a misfortune, and it is doubly a misfortune, because you could have been rich just as well as be poor. Philadelphia furnishes so many opportunities. You ought to be rich. But some people with will ask: "How can spend your time advising the rising generation to give their time to getting money—

钻石就在你身边

dollars and cents—the commercial spirit?"

Yet I must say that you ought to spend time getting rich. You and I know there are some things more valuable than money; of course, we do. Ah, yes! By a heart made unspeakably sad by a grave on which the autumn leaves now fall, I know there are some things higher, grander and sublimer than money. Well does the man know, who has suffered, that there are some things sweeter, holier and more sacred than gold. Nevertheless, the man of common sense also knows that there is not any one of those things that is not greatly enhanced by the use of money. Money is power.

Love is the grandest thing on God's earth, but fortunate the lover who has plenty of money. Money is power; money has power; and for a man to say, "I do not want money," is to say, "I do not

热卖百年的世界级畅销书(最新译本)

wish to do any good to my fellowmen." It is absurd thus to talk. It is absurd to disconnect them. This is a wonderfully great life, and you ought to spend your time getting money, because of the power there is in money. And yet that some people think it is a great honor to be one of God's poor. I am looking in the faces of people who think just that way.

I heard a man once say in a prayer-meeting that he was thankful that he was one of God's poor, and then I silently wondered what his wife would say to that speech, as she took in washing to support the family while he sat and smoked on the veranda. I don't want to see any more of that kind of God's poor. Now, when a man could have been rich just as well, and he is now weak because he is poor, he has done some great wrong; he has been untruthful to himself; he has been

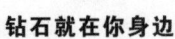
钻石就在你身边

unkind to his fellowmen. We ought to get rich if we can by and Christian methods, and these are the only methods that sweep us quickly toward the goal of riches.

I remember, not many years ago, a young theological student who came into my office and said to me that he thought it was his duty to come in and "labor with me." I asked him what had happened, and he said: "I feel it is my duty to come in and speak to you, sir, and say that the Holy Scriptures declare that money is the root of all evil." I asked him where he found that saying, and he said he found it in the Bible. I asked him whether he had made a new Bible, and he said no, he had not gotten a new Bible, that it was in the old Bible. "Well," I said, "if it is in my Bible, I never saw it. Will you please get the Bible and

热卖百年的世界级畅销书(最新译本)

let me see it?"

He left the room and soon came stalking in with his Bible open, with all the bigoted pride of the narrow sectarian, who founds his creed on some misinterpretation of Scripture, and he puts the Bible down on the table before me and fairly squealed into my ear, "There it is. You can read it for yourself." I said to him, "young man, you will learn, when you get a little older, that you cannot trust another denomination to read the Bible for you." I said, "Now, you belong to another denomination, please read it to me, and remember that you are taught in a school where emphasis is exegesis." So he took the Bible and read it: "The love of money is the root of all evil." Then he had it right.

The Great Book has come back into the esteem and love of the people, and into the respect of the greatest minds of earth, and now you can quote it and rest your life and your death on it without more fear. So, when he quoted right from the Scriptures he quoted the truth. "The love of money is the root of all evil." Oh, that is it. It is the worship of the means instead of the end. Though you cannot reach the end without the means. When a man makes an idol of the money instead of the purposes for which it may be used, when he squeezes the dollar until the eagle squeals, then it is made the root of all evil. Think, if you only had the money, what you could do for your wife, your child, and for your home and your city. Think how soon you could endow the Temple College yonder if you only had the money and the disposition to give it; and yet, my friend, people say you and I should not spend the time getting rich. How inconsistent the whole thing is. We ought to be rich, because money has power.

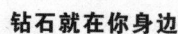

人们对你的评判正是你成功的见证
You can judge your success in others' words about you

我认为,如何变富,这才是我最应该告诉你们的道理,因为我既然告诉你们应该富有,而且我也应该富有,那么我至少应该告诉你们如何才能使自己变得富有。我们之所以对富人有偏见,主要是因为我们时常会被一些有关他们的虚假报道所蒙蔽。人们之所以会编造洛克菲勒先生的谎言,就是因为他拥有巨额的财产——而且有很多人都愿意相信这些谎言。人们对他的报道是多么的荒谬不实呀!而是当许多报纸企图以哗众取宠的报道来扩大销路时，我们却很少能够判断出那些报道是否属实。他们对富人所作的不真实报道的确是一种误导，如果你想把我说的这一点弄明白，那么最好的办法就是去看看目前报纸对费城所作的报道。

前几天，有位年轻人来找我说："如果洛克菲勒先生真像你说的那样是一个好人，为什么还会有那么多人说他的坏话？"那是因为他超越了我们，这就是原因——他超越了我们。为什么安德鲁·卡耐基先生会遭到嫉妒心十足的人们这么严厉的批评？还是因为他所拥有的远比我们多。如果某人知道的比我多，我难道会轻易向他低头屈服而不去攻击他的学识吗？如果某人站在讲坛上演讲，台下有数千人在听，而我的教学班里只有15个人，而且他们还全都睡着了，难道我不会诋毁他吗？事实就是如此，我们通常都会对超越我们的人采取这种行为。为什么你所批评的那个人

钻石就在你身边

拥有1亿元,而你却只有5角钱,而且你们所得的也刚好是你们所值的,这就是差别。

一天,一位大富翁找到我,坐在我的客厅里对我说:"你看到报纸上那些有关我家族的不真实报道了吗?"

"当然,我看到了,而且我一看到那些报道,就知道它们是谎话。"

"他们为什么要这样编造谎言?"

"呵呵,"我对他说,"如果你立即开张1亿元的支票给我,我保证,很快我就可以把这些谎言连同这张支票一起带走。""哎,"他说,"我真看不出他们这样诋毁我和我的家人有什么意义。 康维尔,请你坦诚地告诉我,你认为美国人到底是怎么评价我的?"

"好吧,"我说,"他们认为你是这个世界上有史以来心肠最坏的大恶人!"

"那我该怎么办呢?"他对此无计可施,因为他确实是我所见到过的最虔诚的基督徒之一。事实上，不用大惊小怪，只要你拥有了1亿元的资本，关于你的流言蜚语就自然会伴随着你，从某种程度上来说，你可以从那些关于你的流言蜚语中判断出你成功的程度。所以我觉得你应该做一个富有的人。

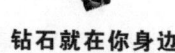

钻石就在你身边

人们对你的评判正是你成功的见证
You can judge your success in others' words about you

I think the best thing for me to do is to illustrate this, for if I say you ought to get rich, I ought, at least, to suggest how it is done. We get a prejudice against rich men because of the lies that are told about them. The lies that are told about Mr. Rockefeller because he has two hundred million dollars—so many people believe them; yet how false is the representation of that man to the world. How little we can tell what is true nowadays when newspapers try to sell their papers entirely on some sensation! The way they lie about the rich men is something terrible, and I do not know that there is anything to illustrate this better than what the newspapers now say about the city of Philadelphia.

A young man came to me the other day and said, "If Mr. Rockefeller, as you think, is a good man, why is it that everybody says so much against him?" It is because he has gotten ahead of us; that is the whole of it—just gotten ahead of us. Why is it Mr. Carnegie is criticized so sharply by an envious world! Because he has gotten more than we have. If a man knows more than I know, don't I incline to criticize somewhat his learning? Let a man stand in a pulpit and preach to thousands, and if I have fifteen people in my church, and they're all asleep, don't I criticize him? We always do that to the man who gets a-

钻石就在你身边

head of us. Why, the man you are criticizing has one hundred millions, and you have fifty cents, and both of you have just what you are worth.

One of the richest men in this country came into my home and sat down in my parlor and said: "Did you see all those lies about my family in the papers?" "Certainly I did; I knew they were lies when I saw them." "Why do they lie about me the way they do?" "Well," I said to him, "if you will give me your check for one hundred millions, I will take all the lies along with it." "Well," said he, "I don't see any sense in their thus talking about my family and myself. Conwell, tell me frankly, what do you think the American people think of me?" "Well," said I, "they think you are the blackest hearted villain that ever trod the soil!" "But what can I do about it?" There is nothing he can do about it, and yet he is one of the sweetest Christian men I ever knew. If you get a hundred million you will have the lies; you will be lied about, and you can judge your success in any line by the lies that are told about you. I say that you ought to be rich.

常识才是你致富最需要的资本
Common sense is the capital for you to be rich

然而在我发表了上述言论之后,就不断有年轻人跑来找我诉苦:"我也很想做生意,可是我却一直办不到。"

"你为什么办不到?"

"我没有资本,怎么开创自己的事业?"

资本,创业的资本?年轻人,你知道你在说什么吗?身在费城,你看看这里的大富翁们吧,他们全都是从穷小子发家的,你还想要什么创业资本!没有资本就是你最大的资本。我真庆幸你没有资本。我十分可怜那些有钱人

热卖百年的世界级畅销书(最新译本)

家的孩子。在现在的社会里,有钱人家的孩子正处于一种非常困难的境地。他们注定要受人怜悯,因为他们永远都无法体会人类生命中那些最宝贵的东西。马萨诸塞州的统计数字告诉我们,每17个有钱人家的孩子中,竟没有一个人在死的时候还是富翁。他们生于富裕,成长于富裕,却死于贫穷。即使一个富人的儿子有幸保住了他父亲的财富,他也同样无法体会生命中最宝贵的东西。

我们学院里的一名年轻人曾经问我,在我看来,人的一生中最快乐的时刻是什么时候?这个问题我研究了很久,最后才得出结论。我认为,在人们所经历的一切事物中,让人感到最快乐的事情,就是一个年轻人第一次抱着他的新娘跨过由他赚钱买来的或是亲手建造的房子的门槛,然后面向他的新娘,以一种用任何语言都难以描述的好口才对他的妻子说道:"亲爱的,我亲手赚来了这栋房子,整栋房子都是我自己赚来的。它完全属于我，现在，我愿意与你共同分享。"这是人类所能感受到的最伟大的时刻了。可是富家子弟却无法体会这一刻的快乐。或许他可以带着新娘住进一幢更漂亮的豪宅，可是当他们走进这栋房子时，他只能说："我母亲给了我这个，给了我那个；我父亲给了我这个，给了我那个。"说到最后，他的妻子甚至开始希望自己嫁的是他父亲而不是他了。

哎，我是多么可怜那些富家子弟呀！他们只知道挥霍金钱，却又得不到什么好下场。你难道没有见过富家子弟在亚特兰大赌场沉沦吗？我的确曾见过这样一个草包，而且我永远也不会忘记他。我当时在尼亚加拉瀑布发表演讲，演讲完毕后，我就准备回旅馆。我刚走到旅店的柜台前时就看到一位百万富翁的儿子正站在那儿，他来自纽约。他可真是难以形容的无能。当时，他正用胳膊肘拄着一根金柄手杖,依我看,那跟手杖的"脑袋"所装的智慧都要比他的头脑所装的多。我想即使我做再多的努力,我都无法将这个年轻人正确地描述出来,我办不到。但我还是要试一试,当时他戴着一副不透明的眼镜,穿着一双令他无法走路的漆皮皮鞋,另外还穿着一条令他无法蹲下的裤子——他打扮的完全就像只蚱蜢!

巧得很,就在我走进旅店时,这位蚱蜢先生也来到了柜台前。他先是扶了扶他那副连眼前景象都看不清的眼镜,因为他说的是印度英语,所以他就咬字不清地对柜台职员说:"天(先)生,天(先)生,能否劳驾你给我一些信主(纸)和信轰(封)!"那位职员迅速打量了他一眼,然后打开一个抽屉,取出一些信纸和信封,之后一把把它们丢在柜台上,又转过头去看他的书了。

当那些信封和信纸被丢到柜台上时,你

钻石就在你身边

可以想象得到那个蚱蜢先生的表情！要知道他想要什么东西，向来都是由仆人双手奉上的。他又扶了一下他那副深色的眼镜，然后在那位职员背后大叫："转过来，天(先)生，把脸转到这边来，天(先)生，能否请你命令一个朴(仆)人，把这些信主(纸)和信轰(封)拿到那边的桌子上去。"哦，他可真是一只可怜、可悲又可恨的美国大猴子。他竟然没法子把信封和信纸拿到 20 尺外的桌子上去。我猜想，可能他连把自己的胳膊从手杖上放下来都做不到。对于这种人类的败类，我一点儿都不同情。所以，如果你没有资本，我真的很替你高兴。你不需要资本，你需要的只是常识，而不是金钱。

常识才是你致富最需要的资本
Common sense is the capital for you to be rich

But there are ever coming to me young men who say, "I would like to go into business, but I cannot." "Why not?" "Because I have no capital to begin on." Capital, capital to begin on! What! Young man! Living in Philadelphia and looking at this wealthy generation, all of whom began as poor boys, and you want capital to begin on? It is fortunate for you that you have no capital. I am glad you have no money. I pity rich men's sons. A rich man's son in these days of ours occupies a very difficult position. They are to be pitied. A rich man's son cannot know the very best things in human life. He cannot. The statistics of Massachusetts show us that not one out of seventeen rich men's sons ever die rich. They are raised in luxury, they die in poverty. Even if a rich man's son retains his father's money, even then he cannot know the best things of life.

A young man in our college yonder asked me to formulate for him what I thought was the happiest hour in a man's history, and I studied it long and came back convinced that the happiest hour that any man ever sees in any earthly matter is when a young man takes his bride over the threshold of the door, for the first time, of the house he himself has earned and built, when he turns to his bride and with an eloquence greater than any language of him, he says to his wife:

热卖百年的世界级畅销书(最新译本)

"My loved one, I earned this home myself; I earned it all. It is all mine, and I share it with you." That is the grandest moment a human heart may ever see. But a rich man's son cannot know that. He goes into a finer mansion with his wife, it may be, but he is obliged to go through the house and say: "My mother gave me this, gave me that; my father gave me this, gave me that," until his wife wishes she had married his father.

Oh, I pity a rich man's son. I do. Until he gets so far along in his dudeism that he gets his arms up like that and can't get them down. Didn't you ever see any of them astray at Atlantic City? I saw one of these scarecrows once and I never tire thinking about it. I was at Niagara Falls lecturing, and after the lecture I went to the hotel, and when I went up to the desk there stood a millionaire's son from New York. He was an indescribable specimen of anthropologic potency. He carried a goldheaded cane under his arm—more in its head than he had in his. I do not believe I could describe the young man if I should try. But still I must say that he wore an eye-glass he could not see through; patent leather shoes he could not walk in, and pants he could not sit down in—dressed like a grasshopper!

Well, this human cricket came up to the clerk's desk just as I came in. He adjusted his unseeing eye-glass in this wise and lisped to the clerk, because it's "Hinglish, you know," to lisp: "Thir, thir, will you have the kindness to furnish me with thome papah and thome envelopehs!" The clerk measured that man quick, and he pulled out a drawer and took some envelopes and paper and cast them across the counter and turned away to his books.

You should have seen that specimen of humanity when the paper and envelopes came across the counter—he whose wants had always been anticipated by servants. He adjusted his unseeing eye-glass and he yelled after that clerk: "Come back here, thir, come right back here. Now, thir, will you order a thervant to take that papah and thothe envelopehs and carry them to yondah dethk." Oh, the poor, miserable, contemptible American monkey! He couldn't carry paper and envelopes in twenty feet. I suppose he could not get his arms down. I have no pity for such travesties of human nature. If you have no capital, I am glad of it. You don't need capital; you need common sense, not copper cents.

钻石就在你身边

满足了人们的需求你就能致富
You will be rich when you know what people need

A.T. 斯图沃特是纽约的顶级大商人，他可以说是他那个时代最富有的美国人，但他却曾经是个穷小子。最初他只带了一元五角钱，就到商海去打拼。而在他刚开始做生意时，他却一下子就赔进去了八角七分五厘，因为他用这些钱买了一些针、线和钮扣出售，可是人们却并不想买这些东西。

你是穷人吗？那是因为你的东西没有人要，你只好把他们压在自己手里却卖不出去。这是一个很好的教训。这个理论你可以随便放在谁的身上都很适用,无论是年轻人,还是老人。斯图沃特不知道人们需要什么,所以他就买了一些人们并不需要的东西,结果砸在自己手里,注定他要亏本。后来,斯图沃特也从中得到了他商业生涯中受益最大的教训,他说:"我再也不会先买进任何东西,只有在我了解人们想要买什么东西之后,我才会去进货。"之后,他便挨家挨户去问人们需要什么东西,在他知道了人们都需要什么东西之后,他才把剩下的六角二分五厘再投资下去,去购进"大家所需要的东西。"我不管你从事什么职业,我也不在乎你是律师、医生、家庭主妇、教师或是其他什么人,这个原则都完全适用。无论做什么,我们必须首先知道这个世界需要什么,然后再进行投资,只有向世人提供他们所需要的东西,成功才能水到渠成。斯图沃特一直坚持遵循这个原则,最后他终于拥有了4000万美元的资产。"可是,"或许你

钻石就在你身边

会这么说,"在纽约想要做到这一点很容易,可是在费城就不行了。"1889年一项通过各种渠道获得的关于纽约富人的详细统计数字显示,当时纽约有107位财产超过1000万美元的千万富翁。这真是出人意料,而且很多人会理所当然地认为他们都是到纽约后才挣到这么多钱的。然而事实上,在那些107位千万富翁中,只有7人是在纽约发家致富的,而其余的100位富人都是在外地发财后,才搬到纽约居住的。更出人意料的是,在这100位富人中,竟然有67位是在人口不足6000的小镇上发财的。而且全美国最富有的人竟然就住在一个人口只有3500人的小镇上,并且一直就住在那儿,从未搬到别处去。所以,你住在哪里并不重要,相反,住在太大的城市倒有可能为你带来诸多不便,所以你一定要记住,成为百万富翁的大机会,就隐藏在较小的城市里。

热卖百年的世界级畅销书(最新译本)

关于这一点,我能举出的最恰当不过的例子就是关于约翰·雅各布·阿斯特的故事。约翰年轻时也是个穷小子,后来他为阿斯特家族赚了大量的财富,而且他所赚的钱远远超过他的任何一位祖先。刚起步时他曾拥有纽约一家女帽店的抵押权,原因是由于原来的店主无法筹到足够的钱支付租金和利息,于是就提前取消了店面赎回的权利,于是阿斯特就拥有了这家女帽店的抵押权,并和原来那位失败的店主合伙经营起这家店来。当时他只是持有店面的股份,并没有为店面投资一分钱,而且他还要原来的那位店主单独看店,自己却跑到公园里,找张椅子坐了下来。也就是在公园的那张椅子上,他进行着从事这项合伙生意中最重要——而且在我看来也是最轻松、最愉快的一部分工作。他坐在那儿打量着来来往往的女士,思索以前那位店主的失误之所在。当一位女士昂首挺胸地从他面前走过时,她是那么的骄傲,好像并不在乎是否整个世界都在看着她,这时,约翰注意到了她头上所戴的软帽。在那位女士尚未从他的视线里消失之前,他已经看清楚并记住了那顶软帽的形状、颜色、花边的式样以及帽子的其他特征。有几次我也曾试着去描述女人所戴的软帽的样式,可是这一点却并不重要,因为到第二天晚上,那顶帽子的式样就要过时了。

  琢磨透那顶软帽的特征后,约翰·雅各布·阿斯特就回到了店里,对那位店主说,"现在请你在橱窗里摆一顶和我所描述的完全一样的软帽,"他说,"因为我刚才看到一位女士很喜欢这种帽子。所以在我回来之前,不要再摆出其他式样的帽子。"说完,他又走了出去,又跑到公园里找张椅子坐了下来。不久又有一位不同身材、不同肤色的女士从他面前走过,当然,她所戴的帽子的颜色和形状也别具风格。于是,他又回到店里对他的店主说:"现在要像刚才那样摆出这样的一款帽子来。"

通过这个方法,他总是能在橱窗里所摆出能够吸引顾客,而不会让顾客看了就掉头走的帽子。而原先那位店主,也不用因为顾客都跑到别的店里去买帽子而到店后头号啕大哭了,相反,之前他在橱窗里摆设的帽子都是他从来都没有见人戴过的。

钻石就在你身边

满足了人们的需求你就能致富
You will be rich when you know what people need

You will be rich when you know what people need

A. T. Stewart, the great princely merchant of New York, the richest man in America in his time, was a poor boy; he had a dollar and a half and went into the mercantile business. But he lost eighty-seven and a half cents of his first dollar and a half because he bought some needles and thread and buttons to sell, which people didn't want.

Are you poor? It is because you are not

wanted and are left on your own hands. There was the great lesson. Apply it whichever way you will it comes to every single peoples' life, young or old. He did not know what people needed, and consequently bought something they didn't want, and had the goods left on his hands a dead loss. A. T. Stewart learned there the great lesson of his mercantile life and said "I will never buy anything more until I first learn what the people want; then I'll make the purchase." He went around to the doors and asked them what they did want, and when he found out what they wanted, he invested his sixty-two and a half cents and began to supply a "known demand." I care not what your profession or occupation in life may be; I care not whether you are a lawyer, a doctor, a housekeeper, a teacher or whatever else, the principle is precisely the same. We must know what

钻石就在你身边

the world needs first and then invest ourselves to supply that need, and success is almost certain. A. T. Stewart went on until he was worth forty million. "Well," you will say, "a man can do that in New York, but cannot do it here in Philadelphia." The statistics very carefully gathered in New York in 1889 showed one hundred and seven millionaires in the city worth over ten million apiece. It was remarkable and people think they must go there to get rich. Out of that one hundred and seven millionaires only seven of them made their money in New York, and the others moved to New York after their fortunes were made, and sixty-seven out of the remaining hundred made their fortunes in towns of less than six thousand people, and the richest man in the country at that time lived in a town of thirty-five hundred inhabitants, and always lived there and never moved

热卖百年的世界级畅销书(最新译本)

away. It is not so much where you are as what you are. But at the same time if the largeness of the city comes into the problem, then remember it is the smaller city that furnishes the great opportunity to make the millions of money.

The best illustration that I can give is in reference to John Jacob Astor, who was a poor boy and who made all the money of the Astor family. He made more than his ancestors have ever earned, and yet he once held a mortgage on a millinery store in New York, and because the people could not make enough money to pay the interest and the rent, he foreclosed the mortgage and took possession of the store and went into partnership with the man who had failed. He kept the same stock, did not give them a dollar of capital, and he left them alone and he went out and sat down upon a bench in the park. Out there on

钻石就在你身边

that bench in the park he had the most important, and, to my mind, the pleasantest part of that partnership business. He was watching the ladies as they by; and where is the man that wouldn't get rich at that business? But when John Jacob Astor saw a lady pass, with her shoulders back and her head up, as if she did not care if the whole world looked on her, he studied her bonnet; and before that bonnet was out of his sight he knew the shape of the frame and the color of the trimmings, the curl of the—something on a bonnet. Sometimes I try to describe a woman's bonnet, but it is of little use, for it would be out of style by tomorrow night.

So John Jacob Astor went to the store and said: "Now, put in the show window just such a bonnet as I describe to you because," said he, "I have just seen a lady who likes just such a bonnet. Do not make up any more till I come back." And he went out again and sat on that bench in the park, and another lady of a different form and complexion passed him with a bonnet of different shape and color, of course. "Now," said he, "put such a bonnet as that in the show window."

He didn't fill his show window with hats and bonnets which drive people away and then sit in the back of the store and bawl because the people go somewhere else to trade. He didn't put a hat or bonnet in that show window the like of which he had not seen before it was made up.

钻石就在你身边

你无法致富是因为你感到沮丧
You can't get rich because you feel depressed

特别是在我们这个城市里,有很多机会生产不同的商品,而且现在工厂里股东和员工的界限划分得十分明显。此外,朋友们,现在美国已经出现了一种令人沮丧又忧郁的气氛,工人们开始感觉到,他们正被头顶上的一种无法冲破的硬壳给压制着,而且那些高高在上的老板们,不仅个个都是伪君子,还绝不会下来帮他们一把。这就是美国广大公民们心里所想的。但是,朋友们,在我们国家的历史上,从来就没有这么好的机会可使一个穷

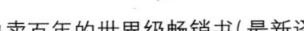
热卖百年的世界级畅销书（最新译本）

人迅速致富，而且目前也再没有比费城机会更大的城市了。而他们真正无法致富的原因就是因为他们觉得丧气,这就是事实的真相。事实上,道路是畅通的,只要努力了,由穷人变成富人的道路还是可是实现通畅的。

我知道工会现在有两个大问题需要解决,而解决这两个问题的办法只有一个。而工会所做的却跟现在的资本家一样,是在极力地阻止对这些问题的解决,而且这显然是同一问题的两个对立面。工会有两大困难要解决:第一,做一个劳动能力的划分,把每一个阶层的劳动者都放在同一标准上,他们把一个每天能赚5美元的工人的工资降为每天赚2.5美元,以便将他和一名一天赚不到0.5美元的低级别的工人置于相同的局面。对于工人而言,这是最危险且最令人泄气的事情。如果一个工人的工作做得比其他人好,或是从事更加高层的工作,或是他的工作时间较长,而他却无法得到他应有的报酬,这是十分危险的事情,想要使每一个美国工人都获得自由,都获得和其他美国人能够完全平等的权利,就不妨让工人自己去要求他们所应该得到的报酬,并让他获得这个报酬——而不是让任何一位雇主对他们说:"你应该替我工作,但你却只能得到你所应得的报酬的一半";更不能让任何一个工会组织说:"你应该替雇主工作,而且你只能拿你应得报酬的一半。"

只有做一个真正的人,一个独立的人,工人们才会发现,从贫穷通往富裕的道路原来是通畅的。

工会的另一个困难就是他们必须自己去考虑的,而且必要时由他们自己去解决的,那就是如何面对那些向他们谈论富人压榨穷人的演讲者。我甚至可以在梦里重述我在这种情况下多次听到的这类演讲辞。我一生都在

和工人一起生活,我自己也是个工人,而且我经常在工人的生产线上,听到被工会邀请的演讲者所作的演说。那些演讲者站在这些忠厚老实的工人面前,然后开口说道:"各位诚实的工业界的工人朋友们,你们为这个世界创造了最多的资本,你们建造了所有的宫殿,修建了所有的铁路,制造了远行于海洋之上的轮船,可是,各位工人朋友们!你们什么都得不到,你们只不过是奴隶,你们受尽了雇主的压榨,而他们却高高骑在你们的脖子之上,在他们豪华的别墅里享乐,他们的保险柜里装满了黄金,你们可知道,他们所拥有的每一块钱,都是通过压榨你们这些诚实的工人所得来的。"这就是工人们时常听到的那种演讲,这些演讲在不停地向人们表明雇主是如此贪婪,工人们是如何百般地被人奴役。

哦,这是多么荒谬的演讲呀!只有那些深爱着自己国家和信仰的人才会殚精竭力、全心全意地想要通过适当的方式来达到工人与雇主相互沟通和联系的目的，而那些极力挑拨雇主和雇工，以及雇工和雇主之间关系的人则别有用心。

热卖百年的世界级畅销书(最新译本)

你无法致富是因为你感到沮丧
You can't get rich because you feel depressed

In our city especially, there are great opportunities for manufacturing, and the time has come when the line is drawn very sharply between the stockholders of the factory and their employees. Now, friends, there has also come a discouraging gloom upon this country and the laboring men are beginning to feel that they are being held down by a crust over their heads through which they find it impossible to break, and the aristocratic money owner–himself is so far above that he will never descend to their assistance. That is the thought in the minds of our people. But, friends, never in the history of our country was there an opportunity so great for the poor men to get rich as there is now and in the city of Philadelphia. The very fact that they get discouraged is what prevents them from getting rich. That is all there is to it. The road is open, and let us keep it open between the poor and the rich. I know that the labor unions have two great problems to contend with, and there is only one way to solve them. The labor unions are doing as much to prevent its solving as are capitalists today, and there are positively two sides to it. The labor union has two difficulties: the first one is that it began to make a labor scale for all classes on a par, and they scale down a man that can earn five dollars a day to two and a half a day, in order to level up to him an imbecile that cannot earn fifty cents a day. That is one of the most dangerous and discouraging things for the working men. He cannot get the results of his work if he do better work or higher work or work longer; that is a dangerous thing, and in order to get every laboring man free and every American equal to every other American, let the laboring man ask what he is worth and get it—not let any capitalist say to him: "You shall work for me for half of what you are worth"; nor let any labor organization say: "You shall work for the capitalist for half your worth."

Be a man, be independent, and then shall the laboring man find the road ever open from poverty to wealth.

The other difficulty that the labor union has to consider, and this problem they have to solve themselves, is the kind of orators who come and

钻石就在你身边

talk to them about the oppressive rich. I can see in my dreams recite the oration I have heard again and again under such circumstances. My life has been with the laboring man. I am a laboring man myself. I have often, in their assemblies, heard the speech of the man who has been invited to address the labor union. The man gets up before the assembled company of honest laboring men and he begins by saying: "Oh, you honest, industrious laboring men, who have furnished all the capital of the world, who have built all the palaces and constructed all the railroads and covered the ocean with her steamships. Oh, you laboring men! You are nothing but slaves; you are ground down in the dust by the capitalist who is gloating over you as he enjoys his beautiful estates and as he has his banks filled with gold, and every dollar he owns is coined out of the heart's blood of the honest laboring man." Now, that is a lie, and you know it is a lie; and yet that is the kind of speech that they are hearing all the time, representing the capitalists as wicked and the laboring man so enslaved.

Why, how wrong it is! Let the man who loves his flag, and believes in American principles endeavor with all his soul to bring the capitalists and the laboring man together until they stand side by side, and arm in arm, and work for the common good of humanity. He is an enemy to his country who sets capital against labor or labor against capital.

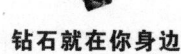
钻石就在你身边

伟大的恰好就是简单的
The greatest just is the simplest

下面假设我走到台下去,走到听众身边,然后请你们给我介绍一位住在费城的大发明家。你们或许会说:"费城的发明家?我们这里哪有什么发明家?发明东西可是件很艰难又耗时的事。"然而事实上,在我们这座城市确实有很多伟大的发明家,而且就在现场的听众席中,就有人曾发明了某种机器,并最终成了发明家,还成了用他们的发明带给全世界人方便的最伟大的发明家,说不定他们就是你们认识的某位先生或是女士,而在他们自己看来，他们却会认为自己不可能发明出任何东西。

不知你们是否研究过发明史？如果你们曾阅读过这些资料，你们就会发现一件很奇怪的事：那些最伟大的发明家，在他们做出伟大的发明之前，从来都没想过自己将来能够成为发明家。那么，谁是伟大的发明家？他们不过是这样一类人：他们心中充满痛苦，有着直觉的常识，可以注意到世界上的某些需求，然后便立即投入全部精力去研究这项需求。所以，如果你想发明任何东西，那就不要凭空猜想，也不要根据你的仪器猜测。相反，你首先要做的就是找出人们需要什么，然后去为满足这种需求而努力，这种方法可以引导你发明出以前你连做梦也想不出来的东西。伟大的发明家大多都是这么简单的伟人。一个人越伟大，他也就越简单；一个人越简单，他也就越伟大；一种机器越简单，它的适用

钻石就在你身边

性就越强,价值也就越大。

不知你们是否认识某位真正伟大的人物?如果认识,你们就会发现他们的为人一般都非常单纯、平易近人、朴实。有时,你们或许会认为,他们所从事的工作是其他任何人都可以做好的。所以,如果你们真的遇上了某位伟大的人物,比如说他刚好是你的邻居,那么你们就可以径直朝他走去,与他打个招呼:"你好,吉姆!你早,山姆。"是的,你完全可以这样做,因为他们一向都如此平易近人。

在我撰写美国加菲尔德将军的平生故事时,我曾去拜访过他。当我到达他家附近时,他的一位邻居热情地将我带到他家后门,然后大声叫道,"吉姆!吉姆!",不一会儿,"吉姆"就出现在了门口,开门请我进去。这就是本世纪最伟大的人物之一——加菲尔德将军。事实上,世界上其他许多伟人也都如此。有一次我前往弗吉尼亚,去拜访一位教育机构的名人,到了当地之后,经人指点,我向一位当时正在剪枝的男士打听道:"你好,我想拜见罗伯特·李将军,他是这所大学的校长。"只见他平静地回答道:"先生,我就是李将军。"确实如此,当你们遇见这样一位人物——如此高贵的一位人物时,你们将会发现,他真的是一个如此平易近人、朴实的人,那些伟人通常都是如此谦逊,那些伟大的发明家也往往如此朴实。

有一次,我在学校一个班里询问学生们,谁是伟大的发明家,一位小女生立即起身回答说:"哥伦布"。很好,她说的不错。哥伦布曾经买下过一个农场,之后他就开始经营着那个农场,就像我曾经营我父亲的农场一样。一天,他拿着一把锄头出门,走累了,他便坐在一块石头上歇脚。而就在他坐在海边眺望远方广阔的海洋时,他突然注意到,船只向外海驶去时,离岸边越远,船身就越向海水深处

钻石就在你身边

"沉"下去,刚好在当时发生了一件西班牙的沉船事故。哥伦布看着船上桅杆的最顶部逐渐沉了下去,直到再也看不到了之后,他联想到:"这个道理就跟他的那把锄头的柄一样,如果你绕着锄头的柄头走一圈,那么你走得越远,相对于锄头的柄头而言你就越往下。这样看来我就可以绕地球航行前往东印度了。"你看,哥伦布作出远航决定的原因就是如此简单。这位伟人的头脑也是如此简单——如同一座高山,既雄伟又简单。通过这些事例,你们就应该明白谁才是伟大的发明家了,他们就是那些简单又平凡的人,他们的过人之处,不过是因为他们能看出人们的需求,然后决心行动去满足人们的需求罢了。

热卖百年的世界级畅销书(最新译本)

伟大的恰好就是简单的
The greatest just is the simplest

Suppose I were to go down through this audience and ask you to introduce me to the great inventors who live here in Philadelphia. "The inventors of Philadelphia," you would say, "why, we don't have any in Philadelphia. It is too slow to invent anything." But you do have just as great inventors, and they are here in this audience, as ever invented a machine. But the probability is that the greatest inventor to benefit the world with his discovery is some person, perhaps some lady, who thinks he or she could not invent anything.

　　Did you ever study the history of invention and see how strange it was that the man who made the greatest discovery did it without any previous idea that he was an inventor? Who are the great inventors? They are people with plain, straightforward common sense, who saw a need in the world and immediately applied themselves to supply that need. If you want to invent anything, don't try to find it in the wheels in your head nor the wheels in your machine, but first find out what the people need, and then apply yourself to that need, and this leads to invention on the part of people you would not dream of before. The great inventors are simply great men; the greater the man the more simple the man; and the more simple a machine, the more valuable it is.

　　Did you ever know a really great man? His

ways are so simple, so common, so plain, that you think any one could do what he is doing. So it is with the great men the world over. If you know a really great man, a neighbor of yours, you can go right up to him and say:"How are you, Jim, good morning, Sam." Of course you can, for they are always so simple.

When I wrote the life of General Garfield, one of his neighbors took me to his back door, and shouted, "Jim, Jim, Jim!" and very soon "Jim" came to the door and General Garfield let me in—one of the grandest men of our century. The great men of the world are ever so. I was down in Virginia and went up to an educational institution and was directed to a man who was setting out a tree. I approached him and said, "Do you think it would be possible for me to see General Robert E. Lee, the President of the University?" He said, "Sir, I am General Lee." Of course, when you meet such a man, so noble a man as that, you will find him a simple, plain man. Greatness is always just so modest and great inventions are simple.

I asked a class in school once who were the great inventors, and a little girl popped up and said: "Columbus." Well, now, she was not so far wrong. Columbus bought a farm and he carried on that farm just as I carried on my father's farm. He took a hoe and went out and sat down on a rock. But Columbus, as he sat upon that shore and looked out upon the ocean, noticed that the ships, as they sailed away, sank deeper into the sea the farther they went. And since that time some other "Spanish ships" have sunk into the sea. But as Columbus noticed that the tops of the masts dropped down out of sight, he said: "That is

热卖百年的世界级畅销书(最新译本)

the way it is with this hoe handle; if you go around this hoe handle, the farther off you go the farther down you go. I can sail around to the East Indies." How plain it all was. How simple the mind—majestic like simplicity of a mountain in its greatness. Who are the great inventors? They are ever the simple, plain, everyday people who see the need and set about to supply it.

钻石就在你身边

你的财富就在你身边
Your wealth is just on your side

之前,有一次我在北卡罗莱纳州演讲,当时在场的听众中有位银行出纳,在他前面刚好坐着一位戴着一顶很大帽子的女士。当我对在座的听众演讲说:"你们可以获得的财富就在你们附近,或许你们现在正盯着你们的财富看呢。"时,这位出纳对坐在身边的朋友耳语说:"如果真是这样的话,那么我的财富就在那顶帽子里了。"之后,他又写信给我提起这件事,我在给他的回信中写道:"人们的需求所能带给人们的财富有时比任何一种矿场所能给人们带来的财富都要多。"他领会了我的构思后,就拟定了一个生产帽子别针的计划,他要生产一种比那天演讲会上他面前那顶帽子上的别针更好的别针,而且现在他所计划的这种新式别针已经开始投入生产。后来他的别针专利还卖了 52 000 美元。这人没出我的演讲大厅,就已经交上了好运。由此看来,想要变富的关键就在于:你能否看到人们的需求?

我清楚地记得很早以前在我老家的山区里有个人,当时他是个彻头彻尾的穷光蛋,因为贫困,他一直靠接受镇上的救济生活了二十多年。他家有一棵枝叶茂密的枫树,那棵枫树枝叶繁茂,刚好笼罩在他家的屋子上方,像是上天对他特别的恩惠。现在我还一直记得那棵树,因为在我小时候,每年春天,总有一群调皮的孩子围着他家那棵枫树。春天时,那个穷人就会把水桶放在枫树的缺口下方,用

钻石就在你身边

来接枫树留下来的汁液,用来制糖。我还清楚地记得那个水桶放在什么地方。那时,和我一样大小的孩子,每天早上在那人尚未起床之前和晚上睡觉之后,就会跑到枫树底下,偷偷地将那些甜甜的枫汁全部喝光。我敢发誓,他们真的是这样做的。

或许就因为如此,那个人虽然也能接到不少枫树汁,可是他却一直没有制造出太多太好吃的枫树糖来。可是有一天,他突然制造出了又白又晶莹剔透的枫树糖。甚至一位去他家串门的客人都不敢相信那种糖是用枫树汁制成的,因为他一直以为,枫树糖应该是红色或黑色的。于是这位客人就建议那个人:"你何不用这种方法把枫树汁全都制成这样的糖?然后卖给糖果店?"后来,那个穷人就采纳了这个建议,制成了"枫树糖块"。而且在他的这个专利权过期之前,他已经靠卖这种糖赚了 90 000 美元,并且还在那棵枫树所

热卖百年的世界级畅销书(最新译本)

在的地方建造了一幢漂亮的宫殿。在拥有那棵枫树40年后的一个早晨,那位老人醒来之后才猛然发现那棵枫树竟能够给他带来这么多的财富。

事实上,我们之中的很多人都站在这样的枫树旁,一直占有着并利用着它们,而且我们还将继续利用它们,可是却一直没有发现它们的价值,因为我们没有发现人们的需求,而这种发现,在各种发现与发明当中,是人类生命中最浪漫的一件事。

之前,我曾收到许多来自美国和英国各地的信件,这些来信都在述说写信人发现了这个或那个事物。去年春天,有一位先生在俄亥俄州出差的时候曾带我去他的大工厂参观,他告诉我,为了建造这座工厂,他花费了68万美元。之后他告诉我说:"当第一次听你的演讲'钻石就在你家后院'时,我还只不过是个一文不名的穷小子,但自从那以后我便

钻石就在你身边

下定决心不再穷苦下去,我决心要发财,这就是我后来努力的成果。"他带我参观的正是他未抵押的财产,近几年来,我在美国各地演讲时,经常碰到这种情形。我举出上面这个例子,并不是为了自我夸耀,而是为了向你们表明,只要你们愿意,你们同样也可以获得成功。同样可以在几年后向我展示你们的收获。

谁才是伟大的发明家?我记得有一个人就是很好的例证。这个人住在马萨诸塞州东部的布鲁克菲尔德,之前他是个鞋匠,失业后,他一直赋闲在家,直到后来,他妻子实在忍不住了,就要他"滚出去"。于是,按照同法律规定的丈夫必须遵循的做法,他只好按照妻子的要求"滚出了家门"。出来以后,他无处可去,只好在自家后院的一个垃圾箱上坐了下来。想想那种情景!他居然落魄到无家可归,只能坐在垃圾箱上安身。就在他坐到垃圾箱上的时候,他无意识地低头望着脚下的一条小溪,这条小溪从他家后院一直流入下游的草场,他突然看见溪中有一条小鳟鱼,正沿着溪流往上游,看到了他,就躲在了岸边。我猜他当时肯定没有想起来泰尼逊的那首优美的诗歌:

哗啦、哗啦,我在流淌,

我要汇入那溢满的河流,

途中,人来人往,

但我都会永流不息。

当时他可没心情去欣赏诗歌,相反在他看到溪中的鳟鱼后,立即从垃圾箱上跳了起来,跑到溪边用手捉住了那条鳟鱼,然后便把它寄送到了乌斯特(麻州中部的一个城市)。不久后,那边回信给他说,如果他能再寄一条同样的鳟鱼,他们将寄给他一张5美元的钞票。事实上,鳟鱼并没有那么值钱,他们这么做不过是想帮助这个穷人。得到回信后,鞋匠

钻石就在你身边

和他的妻子（他们现在已经和好如初并十分和睦了），想到那张即将到手的钞票,于是就一起出去捉另外一条鳟鱼。他们沿着小溪一直往上走到小溪的源头,又往下,一直走到小溪的尽头,可是找遍整条溪流,他们再也没能找到另一条鳟鱼。他们只好失望地回到家里,然后去找牧师寻求帮助。尽管牧师对鳟鱼的繁殖生长情况一无所知,但他还是为他们指出了一条道路。牧师告诉他们："去买本赛斯·格林的书（鱼类养殖的书),你们就会得到自己想要的一切资料。"于是他们就照牧师的话做了,后来他们果然找到了养殖鳟鱼的一切资料。他们发现,鳟鱼每年产3600个卵,一条鳟鱼每年可以长到0.25磅重。照这个速度,4年后,一条小鳟鱼每年可以产出4吨重的鳟鱼。将他们送到市场上出售,每磅可以卖到5角钱。当他们了解到这些之后,一时还难以相信这个事实,可是,如果他们可以从每条鳟鱼身上获得5美元的利润,那么他们就可以挣到很多钱。

于是,他们就分别用煤炭筛和纱窗放在小溪的上下两头,然后就在自家的后院里开始养殖鳟鱼。他们后来搬去了休斯顿。而且从那个时候起,那个穷人逐步发展成了美国鱼类养殖业的权威人物,现在他已经成了华盛顿"美国鱼类委员会"的第二号人物。我举这个例子的目的同样是为了表明:这个人的财富在被发现之前,已经在他家的后院里待了20年之久。直到有一天,他妻子用拖把柄把他赶出家门那天,他才发现了那些财富!我还记得我曾亲自接待过马萨诸塞州新哈姆地方的一位可怜的木匠,他不但失业了,而且穷苦潦倒,他也被妻子扫地出门了。

坐在海滩上,在百无聊赖之余,他不知不觉把一块浮木削成了一串木项链。而且到了晚上,他的两个孩子竟为了争要这个项链而

钻石就在你身边

吵了起来。当他开始削第二串时,他的一个邻居正好经过,就对他说:"既然你手艺这么好,你为什么不去刻些玩具呢?"他回答说:"可是,我不知道该刻些什么样的玩具?"

这就是整个问题的关键所在。邻居对他说:"你何不问问自己的孩子?"他说:"那又有什么用呢?我的孩子喜欢的玩具,别的孩子并不一定会喜欢。"在学校教书时,像他这样的人我经常碰到。第二天早晨,他的儿子从楼上下来时,他便问儿子道:"山姆,你想要什么样的玩具?""我要一辆手推车。"一会儿他的小女儿也下来了,他又问她想要什么玩具,女儿回答说:"我要一个洋娃娃的洗脸盆、一个洋娃娃的推车、一把洋娃娃的雨伞。"然后又说出了一大堆东西,数目之多以至于他一辈子才都做完。于是,这位木匠就在自家的房子里询问自己孩子的需求,然后便开始制作玩具讨孩子们的欢心。

他就是从用小刀雕刻开始，然后创制出了"辛哈姆玩具"。他现在已经是整个新英格兰州最富有的人了，假如关于罗森先生的故事是真实的话，那么他的财富来源，只不过是在自己家里征询自己孩子的意见而已。所以说，你甚至可以不用走出自己的家门，就能知道应该发明或是制作什么东西。每当我讲述这一话题时，总是难以自控地想要多讲一些。

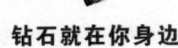

钻石就在你身边

你的财富就在你身边
Your wealth is just on your side

  I was once lecturing in North Carolina, and the cashier of the bank sat directly behind a lady who wore a very large hat. I said to that audience, "Your wealth is too near to you; you are looking right over it." He whispered to his friend, "Well, then, my wealth is in that hat." A little later, as he wrote me, I said: "Wherever there is a human need there is a greater fortune than a mine can furnish." He caught my thought, and he drew up his plan for a better hat pin than was in the hat before him and the pin is now being manufactured. He was offered fifty-two thousand dollars for his patent. That man made his fortune before he got out of that hall. This is the whole question: Do you see a need?

I remember well a man up in my native hills, a poor man, who for twenty years was helped by the town in his poverty, who owned a widespreading maple tree that covered the poor man's cottage like a benediction from on high. I remember that tree, for in the spring—there were some roguish boys around that neighborhood when I was young—in the spring of the year, the man would put a bucket there and the spouts to get the maple sap, and I remember where that bucket was; and when I was young the boys were, oh, so mean, that they went to that tree before that man had gotten out of bed in the morning, and after he had gone to bed at night, and drank up that sweet sap, I could swear they did it.

He didn't make a great deal of maple sugar from that tree. But one day he made the sugar so white and crystalline that the visitor did not believe it was maple sugar; he thought maple sugar must be red or black. He said to the old man: "Why don't you make it that way and sell it for confectionery?" The old man caught his thought and invented the "rock maple crystal," and before that patent expired he had ninety thousand dollars and had built a beautiful palace on the site of that tree. After forty years owning that tree he awoke to find it had fortunes of money indeed in it. And many of us are right by the tree that has a fortune for us, and we own it, possess it, do what we will with it, but we do not learn its value because we do not see the human need, and in these discoveries and inventions that is one of the most romantic things of life. I have received letters from all over the country and from England, where I have lectured, saying that they have discovered this and that, and one man out in Ohio took me through his great factories last spring, and said that they cost him $680,000, and, said he: "I was not worth a cent in the world when I heard your lecture 'Acres of Diamonds'; but I made up my mind to stop right here and make my fortune here, and here it is. "He showed me through his unmortgaged possessions. And this is a continual experience now as I travel through the country, after these many years. I mention this incident, not to boast, but to show you that you can do the same if you will.

Who are the great inventors? I remember a good illustration in a man who used to live in East Brookfield, Mass. He was a shoemaker, and he was out of work and he sat around the house until his wife told him "to go out doors". And he did what every husband is compelled by law to do—he obeyed his wife. And he went out and sat down on an ash barrel in his back yard. Think of it! Stranded on an ash barrel and the enemy in possession of the house! As he sat on that ash barrel, he looked down into that little brook which ran through that back yard into the meadows, and he saw a little trout go flashing up the stream and hiding under the bank. I do not suppose he thought of Tennyson's beautiful poem:

"Chatter, chatter as I flow,

To join the brimming river,

Men may come, and men, may go, but I go on forever."

But as this man looked into the brook, he leaped off that ash barrel and managed to catch the trout with his fingers, and sent it to Worcester. They wrote back that they would give a five dollar bill for another such trout as that, not that it was worth that much, but they wished to help the poor man. So this shoemaker and his wife, now perfectly united, that five-dollar bill in prospect, went out to get another trout. They went up the stream to its source and down to the brimming river, but not another trout could they find in the whole stream; and so they came home disconsolate and went to the minister. The minister didn't know how trout grew, but he pointed the way. Said he: "Get Selh Green's book, and that will give you the information you want."

They did so, and found all about the culture of trout. They found that a trout lays thirty-six hundred eggs every year and every trout gains a quarter of a pound every year, so that in four years a little trout will furnish four tons per annum to sell to the market at fifty cents a pound. When they found that, they said they didn't believe any such story as that, but if they could get five dollars apiece they could make something. And right in that same back yard with the coal sifter up stream and window screen down the stream, they began the culture of trout. They afterwards moved to the Hudson, and since then he has become the authority in the United States upon the raising of fish, and he has been next to the highest on the United States Fish Commission in Washington. My lesson is that man's wealth was out here in his back yard for twenty years, but he didn't see it until his wife drove him out with a mop stick. I remember meeting personally a poor carpenter of Hingham, Massachusetts, who was out of work and in poverty. His wife also drove him out of doors. He sat down on the shore and whittled a soaked shingle into a wooden chain. His children quarreled over it in the evening, and while he was whittling a second one, a neighbor came along and said: "Why don't you whittle toys if you can carve like that?" He said, "I don't know what to make!"

There is the whole thing. His neighbor said to him: "Why don't you ask your own children?" Said he, "What is the use of doing that? My children are different from other people's children." I used to see people like that when I taught in school. The next morning when his boy came down the stairway, he said, "Sam, what do you want for a toy?" "I want a wheelbarrow." When his little girl came down, he asked her what she wanted, and she said, "I want a little doll's wash-stand, a little doll's carriage, a little doll's umbrella." And he went on with a whole lot of things that would have taken his lifetime to supply. He consulted his own children right there in his own house and began to whittle out toys to please them.

He began with his jack-knife, and made those unpainted Hingham toys. He is the richest man in the entire New England States, if Mr. Luwson is to be trusted in his statement concerning such things, and yet that man's fortune was made by consulting his own children in his own house. You don't need to go out of your own house to find out what to invent or what to make. I always talk too long on this subject.

你也能成为伟人
You can also be a great man

我很希望今晚能够在此会晤一些伟大的人物,一些真正伟大的人物!尽管你们会说我们这个城市可没有什么伟大的人物。伟大的人物大都来自伦敦、旧金山、罗马或其他城市——但就不是来自本地——然而,事实上,我们这里伟大的人物和任何其他同规模的城市一样多。或许,在座的听众之中就有许多伟大的人物,有男的,也有女的。

我已经说过,伟大的人物一般都是些十分朴素的人物。因此,此地的大人物和其他城

钻石就在你身边

市的伟大人物一样多。在判断一个人是不是伟大的人物时,我们所犯的最大错误就是,我们总是认为,伟大的人物都应该担任一定的职务。而事实上,世人对什么样的人才是大人物却一无所知。那么什么样的人才是这个世界上伟大的人物呢?

年轻的男女朋友们或许会急于提出这个问题。虽然在一般人的意识里,伟大的人物一般都担任一定的职务,然而事实上却并非如此,伟大的人物未必就非要担任什么职务。而目前当我们在中小学里教导学生时,一般都会说伟大的人物一般都是一些担任高职的人。所以我们必须要尽快转变这种带有偏见的观念,否则这种观念就会成为人们意识的主导而很难改变,这一点毋庸置疑。我们必须教导学生,一个人之所以伟大,在于他本身的价值,而不在于他们所担任的职位。不过,请不要责备那些获得了某种公职便认为自己即将成为大人物的年轻人。

我再请问在座的诸位,你们之中有哪些人打算做个伟大的人物?一名年轻人回答说:"我打算做一个伟大的人物。""那你打算什么时候成为一个伟大的人物?""当我被选出来担任某种公职的时候。"难道你还不明白吗?年轻人,在我们的政府组织形式下,担任公职并没有什么了不起。这是一个民有、民治及民享的政府,一切都是以人民为主,而不是以官员为主,如果这个国家的人们发挥他们应有的治理国家的权力的话,那么,公务员只不过是人民的公仆而已,况且《圣经》上说:"仆人所拥有的没有主人伟大。"

此外《圣经》还指出:"一个执行任务的人,不可能比一个命令他去执行命令的人伟大。"

在我们这个国家,人民才是国家的主人,公务员永远不会比人民更伟大。他们应该是人们的诚实仆人,而不可能是我们之中的伟人。年轻人,请记住,在我们国家,你们从未听说过有哪个人因为担任过任何政治职位而成为伟人,除非他们能够为了国家和人民的利益而牺牲自己的利益。在我们国家,如果让每一个伟人都去担任公职,那将是我们的重大损失。年轻人,请记住:你不可能通过政府的选举而成为伟大的人物。

另一位年轻人说:"总有一天我要成为费城伟大的人物。""这是真的吗?那么你打算何时成为伟大的人物呢?""在另一场战争发生的时候!当我们因为古巴问题或是新泽西问题同墨西哥、英国、俄国、日本、西班牙发生矛盾时,我将在枪林弹雨中冲锋陷阵,将敌国的旗帜从旗杆上扯下,凯旋回国时,我的胸前将挂满勋章,那时候政府会对我委以某项公职来嘉奖我,到时候我就将成为一个伟大的人物!""不,不会的!年轻人,这样做并不是真正的伟大。"但我们不应该责备这位年轻人的此种想法,因为他在高中时接受的就是这种教育,他们的大学历史课本里也是这么写的。他所接受的教育就是,担任公职的人一般都曾经英勇参战过。

我记得,在美国和西班牙战争结束后不久,人们曾在费城举行过一场和平大游行。或许在座的有人会告诉我,那次游行要是发生在现在就好了。当时游行队伍开上布洛街后,那辆载着霍布森的四轮马车就在我家大门口前停下来,所有的人都把他们的帽子抛到半空中,挥舞着手帕,欢呼:"霍布森万岁!"我想,如果我当时在场,估计也会这样大叫,因为他应该获得他的国家赋予他的更大的荣誉和尊重。但是,如果我明天到高中课堂上去问学生:"各位小伙子,是谁击沉梅里马克号的?"如果他们回答:"是霍布森"。那么他们所告诉我的答案当中,就存在7/8的

钻石就在你身边

不实之处,因为击沉梅里马克号的共有8个人,另外7个人由于职位的关系,只能呆在西班牙战场上,而霍布森因为是军官,所以他可以离开战火而回到祖国,接受人民赋予他的荣誉。

朋友们,虽然今晚在座的听众都是知识分子,但我敢说,你们当中很少有人能够说得出和霍布森在一起击沉梅里马克号的另外7个人的姓名。我们为什么要用这种方式来教历史呢?我们必须教导学生,不管一个人的职位多么低微,只要他能够恪尽职守,做好自己的工作,那么美国人民颁给他的荣誉就应该和人民颁给一位国王的荣誉一样。我们的教导方式和一位纽约母亲教导她小儿子的方式一样,当她的小儿子问她:"妈妈,那座高大建筑物是什么?""那是格兰特将军的坟墓。""格兰特将军是谁?""就是那位平定了叛乱的人。"难道历史就应该这么教吗?

热卖百年的世界级畅销书（最新译本）

试想想，如果只有格兰特将军一个人，我们会打胜仗吗？很显然，不会的。那么，为什么要在哈得逊河上造一座坟墓？为什么？这并不是因为格兰特将军本人是位伟大的人物，坟墓之所以建在那儿，是因为他是平定叛乱的代表人物，他代表了20万名为国捐躯的战士，而且在这些战士中许多人都和格兰特同样伟大。这就是那座美丽的坟墓耸立在哈得逊河的真正原因。

我记得有件事可以用来说明这个道理，这也是我今晚所能想到的唯一的例证。虽说提到此事，我会深感惭愧，但我从不敢将它忘掉。现在，我要闭上眼睛，将思绪追溯到1863年，我可以看到位于伯克郡山的我的老家，我看到在牛展示会场上挤满了人，我还看到当地的教堂和市政厅里也都挤满了人，并且我还能听到乐队的演奏，看到国旗飞扬，人们挥舞着彩带，现在看来，我对那天的情景至今记忆犹新。

这些人是前来迎接一连凯旋而归的士兵的,当时,那连的士兵也刚好列队前来。他们已在内战中服完一期的兵役,而且还延长了一期,现在他们正受到家乡父老的迎接。我当时只不过是个年轻小伙子,但我却是那一连的连长。那天,我意气风发,像一个吹足了气的气球——只要一根细细的小针,就可以将我扎破。

我走在队伍的前方,我几乎成了世界上最骄傲的人了。我们列队进入市政厅,人们把我们连的士兵安排在了大厅中央就坐,之后,我就在前排座位上坐了下来,接着,镇上的官员挤过大厅里拥挤的人群走到台上,在台上围成半圆形坐下,稍后担任新英格兰行政委员会会长的本市市长在那个半圆形中央的位子上坐下来。

他是一位头发已经变得灰白的老人,以

前从未担任过公职。他认为，只要他担任了一项公职，他就可以成为一个真正伟大的人物。当他站起来时，他先是调整了一下他那副厚重的眼镜，之后他以无比威严的目光扫视了一遍台下的群众，然后，就将目光落在了我身上，紧接着这位好心的老人就走到台前，示意邀请我到台上来和那些镇上的官员坐在一起。他竟然会邀请我上台！要知道，在我从军之前，从来就没有任何一位市府官员注意过我。有件事或许我现在不该说，不过，我没有任何其他的意思，只是想说明一下事实。当时台上的一位市府官员在我入伍之前曾经建议我的老师把我"刷"掉。

但不论怎么说，我还是应邀上了台，和那些官员坐在一起。我坐在座位上，让我的佩剑垂在地板上，然后双手交叉抱在胸前，等待着接受乡亲们的欢迎。我觉得自己当时就像拿破仑五世！骄傲总在毁灭与失败之前出现。等我坐定之后,大厅里所有的人员都立即安静了下来,厅内鸦雀无声,那位行政委员会主席站了起来,然后以极为威严的姿态走到讲台前。大家都以为他会将镇上的牧师介绍给大家,并告诉大家由牧师代表大家对凯旋归来的士兵致欢迎词,因为牧师是镇上唯一一位演讲者。

但是,朋友们,你们应该能够想象得到当时在场的民众是多么的惊讶,因为他们发现,这位担任市长的老农夫竟然决定由他自己致欢迎词,他以前可从未发表过任何演说,他犯了一项跟别人相同的错误,他似乎认为只要能够成为一名官员,他就可以成为一名演说者,就能发表演说。为此,之前他就写好了一篇演讲词,随后在牧场里踱来踱去地大声朗读,直到完全记住为止。我想,当时牧场里的牛群一定被他的这些举动给吓着了。背完后他便把那篇演讲稿放在了口袋里。现在他又从口袋里把它又拿了出来，之后又小心翼翼地把它摊开在讲桌上。然后，他又调整了一下眼镜，以确定他真能清楚地看到演讲稿上的字。随后他便向后退了几步，接着又威严地走向前去。我想他一定很用心地研究过演讲术，因为他采用的完全是演说家的方式，他将身体的重心放在脚后跟上，两肩后垂，右脚轻轻向前迈进，然后以45度角伸出他的右手臂，展开演讲稿。

他就是以这种演说家的姿态站在台上开始发表演说的，确实如此。有些朋友问我是否太夸张了，我告诉他们我一点儿都不夸张。

真是不可思议，他就用那种姿态开始并进行了他的演讲，不过，我今天不是专门来讲这个故事的，我所要说的是这件事所能带给我们的教训。

"各位亲爱的市民，"他一听到自己的声音，两只手就开始同声音一样颤抖起来，两个膝盖也随之哆嗦起来,接着就是全身发抖。他连同咳嗽带喘气地努力看着演讲稿。然后他又开口说道:"各位亲爱的市民,我们——我们——我们——我们非常高兴——我们非常高兴——我们非常高兴——欢迎这些英勇参战、不畏流血的战士回到他们的故乡——回到他们的故乡。我们尤其——我们尤其——我们尤其——我们尤其高兴,在今天看到跟我们在一起的,还有一位年轻的英雄(指的就是我)——这位年轻的英雄,在想象中(朋友,记住,他确实是说"在想象中",因为如果他不是这样说的,我也不会自负到非要提到这件事)——这位年轻的英雄,在想象中,我们可以看到他曾经率领——我们可以看到他率领部队冲锋陷阵,与敌人进行殊死搏击。我们可以看到他那把闪亮——他那把闪亮——我们可以看到他那把闪亮——他那把闪亮的佩剑——在阳光下发出耀眼的光芒,他对着部

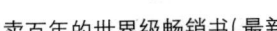

队大叫,'冲啊!'"。哦,天呀,天呀,天呀!这位好心的小老头对战争的认识真是少得可怜。只要他对战争稍有了解,他就应该知道一些当时在座的士兵们都知道的事实,一位步兵军官在危险时跑到部队前面去,那几乎等于犯了大错。我怎么可能手握在阳光下闪闪发光的指挥刀,对我的部下大叫:"冲啊!"我从来都没有这样做过。你想,我会跑到最前面去,然后被前面的敌人和后面的部队前后夹击吗?军官是不应该跑到那地方去的。在实际战斗中,军官的位置就在士兵后面。身为参谋,当叛军从林中冲出,呼喊吼叫着向我方攻来时,我经常要骑着马沿我军防线一路喊道:"军官退后!军官退后!"然后,每一位军官都要退到战线后面,而且军衔越高,就得退得越远。并不是因为他们胆小怕死,而是因为战争的规则要求他们必须这么做。如果将军跑到前线去,然后被打死了,那么这场仗也就必输无疑,因为整个作战计划都在他脑中,所以他必须呆在绝对安全的地方。

我拿着那把"在阳光下闪闪发光的佩剑"。啊!那天坐在市政厅的士兵当中,有人曾冒死保护我这名芝麻般大小的军官,有人背着我横渡极深的河流。而有的人却不在场,因为他们已经为国捐躯了。演讲的人虽然也曾提到过他们,但他却没有注意到他们的价值,即使如此,他们也已经为国家牺牲了,他们为了自己认为是正确的信仰牺牲了。虽然我认为他们更应该受到这样的待遇,可是,这些真正为国牺牲的人却并未受到注意,而我这么一个毛头小子却被当成英雄。

我为什么会被当作英雄?原因很简单,因为那位演讲者也犯了同样愚蠢的错误。这位年轻人是军官,而其余的只是士兵。我由此便得到了终生都难以忘怀的一个教训。一个人之所以伟大,不是因为他拥有什么样的官衔,而是因为他用很少的本钱做出了较大的成绩，以默默无闻的平民身份实现了远大的人生目标，这才是真正的伟大。

一个人只要能够向大众提供更宽阔洁净的街道，更舒适豪华的住宅，更优雅的学校，更庄严的教堂，只要一个人活得更虔诚、更幸福、更善良，那么他就应该得到他所居住的社区民众的感激和祝福，相反一个对自己所在的社区没有做出任何贡献的人，无论他搬到哪里，他都不是一个伟大的人。"我们生活的意义在于行动，而不在于时间长短；在于生活的感受，而不在于重复一些事；在于思想，而不在于仅仅活着，我们应该在正确目标指引下，用心跳的速度来计算时间。"著名作家贝利曾经说："善于思考的人，生活过得最充实。"

如果你忘掉了我今晚所说的全部内容，我希望你也不要忘掉这一点，因为在这短短的几句话中所包含的意义及道理，远远超过

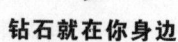
钻石就在你身边

我今天所说的全部内容。贝利说:

"思考最多的人,生活最充实,思想最高贵的人,行为最伟大。"

热卖百年的世界级畅销书（最新译本）

你也能成为伟人
You also can be a great man

I would like to meet the great men who are here tonight. The great men! We don't have any great men in Philadelphia. Great men! You say that they all come from London, or San Francisco, or Rome, or Manayunk, or anywhere else but there—anywhere else but Philadelphia—and yet, in fact, there are just as great men in Philadelphia as in any city of its size. There are great men and women in this audience.

Great men, I have said, are very simple men.

钻石就在你身边

Just as many great men here as are to be found anywhere. The greatest error in judging great men is that we think that they always hold an office. The world knows nothing of its greatest men. Who are the great men of the world? The young men and young women may ask the question. It is not necessary that they should hold an office, and yet that is the popular idea. That is the idea we teach now in our high schools and common schools, that the great men of the world are those who hold some high office, and unless we change that very soon and do away with that prejudice, we are going to change to an empire. There is no question about it. We must teach that men are great only on their intrinsic value, and not on the position they may incidentally happen to occupy. And yet, don't blame the young men saying that are going to be great when they get into some official position.

I ask this audience again who of you are going to be great? Says the young man: "I am going to be great." "When are you going to be great?" "When I am elected to some political office." Won't you learn the lesson, young man; that it is prima facie evidence of littleness to hold public office under our form of government? Think of it. This is a government of the people, and by the people, and for the people, and not for the officeholder, and if the people in this country rule as they always should rule, an officeholder is only the servant of the people, and the Bible says that "the servant cannot be greater than his master."

The Bible says that "he that is sent cannot be greater than he who sent him." In this country the people are the masters, and the officeholders can never be greater than the people, but they are not our greatest men. Young man, remember that you never heard of a great man holding any political office in this country unless he took that office at an expense to himself. It is a loss to every great man to take a public office in our country. Bear this in mind, young man, that you cannot be made great by a political election.

Another young man says, "I am going to be a great man in Philadelphia some time." "Is that so? When are you going to be great?" "When there comes another war! When we get into difficulty with Mexico, or England, or Russia, or Japan, or with Spain again over Cuba, or with New Jersey, I will march up to the cannon's mouth, and amid the glistening bayonets I will tear down their flag from its staff, and I will come home with stars on my shoulders, and hold every office in the gift of the government, and I will be great." "No, you won't! No, you won't; that is no evidence of true greatness, young man." But don't blame that young man for thinking that way; that is the way he is taught in the high school. That is the way history is taught in college. He is taught that the men who held the office did all the fighting.

I remember we had a Peace Jubilee here in Philadelphia soon after the Spanish War. Perhaps some of these visitors think we should not have had it until now in Philadelphia, and as the great procession was going up Broad Street I was told that the tally-ho coach stopped right in front of my house, and on the coach was Hobson, and all the people threw up their hats and swung their handkerchiefs, and shouted "Hurrah for Hobson!" I would have yelled too, because he deserves much more of his country that he has ever received. But suppose I go into the high school tomorrow and ask, "boys, who sunk the Merrimac?" If they answer me "Hobson," they tell me seven-eighths of a lie—seven-eighths of a lie, because there were eight men who sunk the Merrimac. The other seven men, by virtue of their position, were continually exposed to the Spanish fire while Hobson, as an officer, might reasonably be behind the smoke-stack.

Why, my friends, in this intelligent audience gathered here tonight, I do not believe I could find a single person that can name the other seven men who were with Hobson. Why do we teach history in that way? We ought to teach that however humble the station a man may occupy, if he does his full duty in his place, he is just as much entitled to the American people's honor as is a king upon a throne. We do teach it as a mother did her little boy in New York when he said, "Mamma, what great building is that?" "That is General Grant's tomb." "Who was General Grant?" "He was the man who put down the rebellion." Is that the way to teach history?

Do you think we would have gained a victory if it had depended on General Grant alone. Oh, no. Then why is there a tomb on the Hudson at all? Why, not simply because General Grant was personally a great man himself, but that tomb is there because he was a representative man and represented two hundred thousand men who went down to death for this nation and many of them as great as General Grant. That is why that beautiful tomb stands on the heights over the Hudson. I remember an incident that will illustrate this, the only one that I can give tonight. I am ashamed of

钻石就在你身边

it, but I don't dare leave it out. I close my eyes now; I took back through the years to 1863; I can see my native town in the Berkshire Hills, I can see that cattle show ground filled with people; I can see the church there and the town hall crowded, and hear bands playing, and see flags flying and handkerchiefs streaming—well do I recall at this moment that day.

The people had turned out to receive a company of soldiers, and that company came marching up on the Common. They had served out one term in the Civil War and had reenlisted, and they were being received by their native townsmen. I was but a boy, but I was captain of that company, puffed out with pride on that day—why, a cambric needle would have burst me all to pieces.

As I marched on the Common at the head of

my company, there was not a man more proud than I. We marched into the town hall and then they seated my soldiers down in the center of the house and I took my place down on the front seat, and then the town officers filed through the great throng of people, who stood close and packed in that little hall. They came up on the platform, formed a half circle around it, and the mayor of the town, the "chairman of the selectmen" in New England, took his seat in the middle of that half circle.

He was an old man, his hair was gray; he never held an office before in his life. He thought that an office was all he needed to be a truly great man, and when he came up he adjusted his powerful spectacles and glanced calmly around the audience with amazing dignity. Suddenly his eyes fell upon me, and then the good old man came right forward and invited me to come up on the stand with the town officers. Invited me up on the stand! No town officer ever took notice of me before I went to war. Now, I should not say that. One town officer was there who advised the teachers to "whale" me, but I mean no "honorable mention."

So I was invited up on the stand with the town officers. I took my seat and let my sword fall on the floor, and folded my arms across my breast and waited to be received. Napoleon the Fifth! Pride appear before destruction and a fall. When I had gotten my seat and all became silent through the hall, the chairman of the selectmen arose and came forward with great dignity to the table, and we all supposed he would introduce the Congregational minister, who was the only orator in the town, and who would give the oration to the returning soldiers.

But, friends, you should have seen the surprise that ran over that audience when they discovered that this old farmer was going to deliver that oration himself. He had never made a speech in his life before, but he fell into the same error that others have fallen into, he seemed to think that the office would make him an orator. So he had written out a speech and walked up and down the pasture until he had learned it by heart and frightened the cattle, and he brought that manuscript with him, and, taking it from his pocket, he spread it carefully upon the table. Then he adjusted his spectacles to be sure that he might see it, and walked far back on the platform and then stepped forward like this. He must have studied the subject much, for he assumed an elocutionary attitude; he rested heavily upon his left

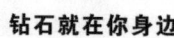
钻石就在你身边

heel, slightly advanced the right foot, threw back his shoulders, apened the organs of speech, and advanced his right hand at an angle of forty-five.

As he stood in this elocutionary attitude this is just the way that speech went, this is it precisely. Some of my friends have asked me if I do not exaggerate it, but I could not exaggerate it.

Impossible! This is the way it went; although I am not here for the story but the lesson that is back of it:

"Fellow citizens." As soon as he heard his voice, his hand began to shake like that, his knees began to tremble, and then he shook all over. He coughed and choked and finally came around to look at his manuscript. Then he began again: "Fellow citizens: We—are—we are—we are—we are—We are—We are very happy—we are very happy—we are very happy—to welcome back to their native town these soldiers who have fought and bleed—and come back again to their native town. We are especially—we are especially—we are especially—we are especially pleased to see with us today this young hero (that meant me this young hero who in imagination (friends, remember, he said 'imagination,' for if he had not said that, I would not be egotistical enough to refer to it) this young hero who, in imagination, we have seen leading his troops—leading—we have seen leading—we have seen leading his troops on to the deadly breach. We have seen his shining—his shining—we have seen his shining—we have seen his shining—his shining sword—flashing in the sunlight as he shouted to his troops, 'Come on!'" Oh dear, dear, dear, dear! How little that good, old man knew about war. If he had known anything about war, he ought to have known what any soldier in this audience knows is true, that it is next to a crime for an officer of infantry ever in time of danger to go ahead of his men. I, with my shining sword flashing in the sunlight, shouting to my troops: "Come on." I never did it. Do you suppose I would go ahead of my men to be shot in the front by the enemy and in the back by my own men? That is no place for an officer. The place for the officer is behind the private soldier in actual fighting. How often, as a staff officer, I rode down the line when the rebel cry and yell was coming out of the woods, sweeping along over the fields, and shouted, "Officers to the rear! Officers to the rear!" and then every officer goes behind the line of battle, and the higher the officer rank, the farther behind he goes. Not because he is any the less brave, but because the laws of war require that to be done. If the general came

热卖百年的世界级畅销书(最新译本)

up on the front line and were killed you would lose your battle anyhow, because he has the plan of the battle in his brain, and must be kept in comparative safety.

I, with my "shining sword flashing in the sunlight." Ah! There sat in the hall that day men who had given that boy their last hardtack, who had carried him on their backs through deep rivers. But some were not there; they had gone down to death for their country. The speaker mentioned them, but they were but little noticed, and yet they had gone down to death for their country, gone down for a cause they believed was right and still believe was right, though I grant to the other side the same that I ask for myself. Yet these men who had actually died for their country were little noticed, and the hero of the hour was this boy.

钻石就在你身边

Why was he the hero? Simply because that man fell into the same foolishness. This boy was an officer, and those were only private soldiers. I learned a lesson that I will never forget. Greatness consists not in holding some office; greatness really consists in doing some great deed with little means, in the accomplishment of vast purposes from the private ranks of life, that is true greatness.

He who can give to this people better streets, better homes, better schools, better churches, more religion, more of happiness, more of God, he that can be a blessing to the community in which he lives tonight will be great anywhere, but he who cannot be a blessing where he now lives will never be great anywhere on the face of God's earth. "We live in deeds, not years, in feeling, not in figures on a dial; in thoughts, not breaths; we should count time by heart throbs, in the cause of right." Bailey says, "He most lives who thinks most."

If you forget everything I have said to you, do not forget this, because it contains more in two lines than all I have said. Baily says:

"He most lives who thinks most, who feels the noblest, and who acts the best."

后记：我的故事

要把它看成是我的一部自传！这是多么奢侈的要求！假如说这里面我所说的都是真实的事件，那么这些关于我生平的故事就显得不那么有趣了。这些看起来单调、枯燥的故事我想应该没有人愿意去读。所以就我自己来讲，我看不出这本书有什么值得夸耀的地方，也看不到自己说了哪些对人们有帮助的东西。它只是我盲目地收集一些与我工作有关的文章组合成的一本书，或者说是一个报道，是一次演讲，再或者只是一则报纸短评或是说明，是一篇杂志专论，虽然这其中有许多故事都可以很容易地在我的图书室里找到。但是我还是觉得，那些关心我的读者们太宽容了，虽然我的工作做得这么草率，但是他们还是给予了不坏的评价。在我看来,除了这颗负担过重的头脑中有一些记忆之外,我实在找不出什么内容来充当自己自传的基础。

近半个世纪在演讲台上的经历,是我珍贵而美好的回忆,每每想起这些我都禁不住会由衷地想要感谢那些给予了我太多祝福和好评的人们,他们所给予我的已经远远超过了我应得的,这使我所获得的成功比我所期望的要多很多;我发现现在年轻人对财富的狂热要比想象中的好很多;而我自己所做的微薄的努力所带来的影响也比我所预料的要大很多。而实际上,我所写的传记大部分也不过是对人们所给我的支持和肯定的叙述。

我亲身经历的成就远远超出了我的想象,为此我常常觉得我的事业好像在被数以千计的手推动着,之后它便神速般的从我身边飞过,最后把我远远地抛在身后。对我来说现实就像一场梦。让我衷心地祝福那些充满爱心和思想高尚的人们吧,他们可以为了别人的利益而选择牺牲自己,却从不计较。所以在我心中

钻石就在你身边

他们中的很多人的精神已经上升到了光明磊落的地步了,而我却一直一个人在日子的流逝中保持沉默,直到自己慢慢地变老。

50年前当我第一次在讲台上演讲时,我还是个热血沸腾的年轻人。当1861年至1865年的内战伴随着爱国主义激情、不安与恐惧来临的时候,我还在耶鲁大学学习法律。很小的时候,我就渴望长大后能够成为一名牧师,那是我的父亲给我最早的关于理想的启蒙。我还记得小时候父亲在伯克郡山的汉普郡高地的小村庄里所做的家庭祷告。他用一种近似呜咽的声音呼唤着上帝:让我像救世主一样对人们做一些特殊的贡献吧。当时的我对父亲充满了敬畏、忧虑和恐惧,直到我决定用自己全部的力量去战胜这种感觉,我才觉得自己得以解脱了。为此,我可以找到各种充分的理由去选择除了传教士之外的其他职业。

然而,当我站在讲台上面对同学们发言而感到紧张、害羞时,当我害怕面对观众时,我的内心里产生了一种奇怪的想法,这种想法促使我想要战胜一直困扰着我的在公众面前演讲时的怯懦。为了战争而招募新兵的公开大会为我提供了实现这种想法的机会。最后我终于在攻打联邦的战役之中做了我生平的第一篇演讲——《历史的教训》。

那真是一个由小男生所做的十分愚蠢的演讲,那是在约翰·高——一位无敌的演说家的极力推荐下,我才有幸站在了马萨诸塞西域的小听众们面前。那是在1862年,暂且不谈演讲本身怎么样,至少从那次以后高先生对我温和的称赞还有听众们的鲜花和掌声使我感到,在公众面前演讲并没有我所想象的那样困难。

从那以后,我开始遵循高先生的提议,尽可能地接受我所收到的每一份演讲邀请,在公众面前谈论各类话题,借此来进行演讲练习。虽然在这段演讲经历中也曾有过许多失败和伤心的眼泪,但是至少我开始觉得我也可以做一个不错的牧师了,我的朋友们也为我的改变而感到高兴。那时我的演说范围包括同学们的野餐、名人的葬礼、周末学校爱国主义集会、周年纪念、毕业典礼、辩论会、牛展览会、缝纫圈等。虽然这些演说都没有任何酬金，但是我还是欣然接受了，并努力地做好每一次演讲。我想在最初的5年里，我所收获的就应该算是经验吧。后来，人们开始偶尔送我一些赠品，类似一把杰克刀、一根火腿或是一本书之类的礼物。演讲为我赢得的第一笔酬金来自一个农民俱乐部，这笔酬金共计75美金，我当时演讲的题目是《马租》。巧的是那个俱乐部的一个成员后来搬到了盐湖城，还成了摩门教会委员会的一名成员。1817年，作为一名记者，我正在做环球旅行，恰好又遇到了他，之后被摩门教会请去演讲，当时我做的是题目为《山脉上的英雄》这篇演讲，这个演讲的酬金是500美元。

所幸的是，在我练习演讲的最初几年里，我曾被聘做过战士、通讯员、律师、编辑，或是牧师等各种有益的职业，这些职业为我带来的收入还算是可以维护我日常的开支。这就使我在这50年的演讲生涯中，很少将演讲酬金用在自己的花销上，相反，我将所有的演讲收入都捐献给了慈善事业。如果说我已经到了可以写一篇自传的年龄上了,那么,以我的作品《钻石就在你家后院》每年被演说 200 多次,而且平均每次演讲的收入是 150 美元的成绩,我应该就不会被人们认为是一个自负的家伙了。

詹姆斯·瑞帕恩先生是著名的竖琴演奏家约翰·布朗先生的传记作者,而布朗先生一直是我父亲的好友,我在学生时代,在假期里就常常靠卖约翰·布朗的传记而赚钱。当他建立起他的第一个演讲所时,而我又有幸被邀请做演讲,这对我来说真是莫大的荣幸。之后我与瑞帕恩先生的交情一直持续到他去世。而我与瑞帕恩先生的结识却要感谢查尔斯·泰勒上校。当时我和他都是波士顿旅行者周刊的记者,是他无私地把我推荐给了瑞帕恩先生,并声称我"有能力将他人无法获得的伟大见解注入到每一个小镇的空虚之处"。每当回忆起查尔斯·泰勒上校,他那具有自我牺牲精神的友谊,都会让我感到十分温暖。

在瑞帕恩先生早期的演讲者的名单中,罗列着很多光辉而伟大的名字:亨利·伍德·贝克,约翰·高,参

钻石就在你身边

议员查尔斯·萨纳,西奥多·蒂尔顿,万德·菲利普斯,玛丽·利物麦夫人,巴亚德·泰勒,拉尔夫·沃尔多·爱默生,他们个个都是当时的伟人,他们要么是大牧师,要么是音乐家,要么是作家。甚至还包括豪默斯博士,约翰·威迪,亨利·朗凡劳,约翰·劳斯罗普·莫特利,乔治·威廉·科迪斯。伯恩塞德上校也被瑞帕恩先生请来过一次或几次,当然他们所做的演讲也都是拒绝任何报酬的。当我看到我的名字出现在这些伟人中间时,我虽然感到有些难为情,但是我还是抑制不了内心的兴奋和激动。我敢肯定,当时认识我的每一个人肯定都在背后嘲笑我。虽然如此,我还是收到了巴亚德·泰勒先生从讲坛大楼寄给我的一封十分友好的信,信中他还说很喜欢我演讲的《伟大的价值之路》。马萨诸塞州的克莱福林市长也抽时间给我寄来了祝贺信。本杰明·巴特上校还鼓励我一定要坚持为做一名优秀的牧师而努力。

演讲的工作对我来说更像是一项任务、一种职责。在从事这份工作的过程中,我从来都没有想过试图去成为一名表演者。我确信,如果不是我一直认为自己想要在演讲中传播一些人生道理,那么,我一定会是一个失败的演说家。所以当我于1879年终于成为一名牧师之后,我便早已经与演讲台非常熟悉了,而且我也早已经明白自己真的没有理由去放弃这样一个伟大而有价值的领域。

在我所有成功的演说中,我所经历的过程基本上都十分类似。每次去做演讲时所经过的道路都是那么的不平坦。不过坎坷的道路、简陋的旅馆、迟到的火车、寒冷的大厅、炎热的教会礼堂、好客的委员会、过度的热情、被打断的梦乡等等,这些烦恼从来都不会在我的记忆中长留,因为我很快就会因为遇到许许多多智慧的面孔,听到很多感谢的呼声和对年轻大学生们的赞助而感到快乐和满足。

在经历过50年的奔波劳碌后,我常被人们问及在乘坐各种交通工具中,我是否遇到过什么事故。的确,要说这些事故从来都没有发生在我身上过,真是一个奇迹。在这其中的27年间,我曾连续不断地每三

钻石就在你身边

天做两次演讲,虽然时间安排得这么紧张,可是却从来没有错过一次演讲。有时,为了赶时间我不得不租用一个专列,但最终我都能按时到达,只有在极个别情况下我会迟到几分钟。在火车和轮船上在我到来之前或离开之后都曾发生过各种事故,有时一些事故就在我眼前发生。所幸的是我从未因此而受过任何伤害。记得有一次要在约翰镇的洪水区做演讲,我在大西洋一个废弃的汽船上停留了26天。还有一次在火车上,一名男子被杀死在卧铺上,而这件事就发生在我离开的半小时后,而之前我刚好就坐在那个铺位上。有时,我真的感觉火车要脱离轨道了,但是最终大家都平安无事。路途中也曾有几个歹徒威胁过我的生命,但最终的结果都是平安无事。

然而,这段时间我的演讲所取得的成果在我看来并没有什么值得炫耀的。相形之下我却觉得自己所做的另一件事更有意义。许多年前,在费城的礼拜堂成员还不到3000人的时候,我就曾成功地说服了这些成员每年捐献出6万美元来鼓舞人道主义精神。这确实是令我感到惊奇的事。在这些钱的资助下慈善医院以惊人的速度扩大，还有阁楼医院的药房帮助生病的、穷苦人们的能力也在不断增强，它们每年都能用高超的技术来帮助成百上千个来此寻求帮助的穷人。做这件事让我感觉到在演讲之外，还有一部分人在我的鼓励下每一小时、每一分钟，都在真诚地行善。坦普大学在仅仅建立 27 年后，所获得的回报已经开始在不断地增加了，一些伟人开始在这里长成——将近十万名青年男女都在这所学校里获得了良好的教育。这所信誉好又不计较经济利益的学校现在已经吸纳了 253 名教授为之效力。对此，我真的觉得可以对之加以赞颂。而我在这篇传记里提到这所学校，仅仅是想写一些在我 50 年时间的演讲工作之外的东西。

而我最为人所熟知的演讲《钻石就在你家后院》，仅仅起源于一次偶然的演说。它是我在与内战期间马萨诸塞第 46 兵团的老战友们（当时我是陆军上校）重新团聚时所作的。当时我从未想过要重做这个演说，甚至在演讲委员会提出这个要求之后，我也没有想要

钻石就在你身边

继续去演讲,因为我一贯如此,从不喜欢做重复的演讲。之后这个演说又重复了大约 5000 次。至于它为什么如此受欢迎,我想我永远都无法给自己或是他人一个合理的解释。我常常抱着"这是一次行善的机会"的想法试图去使自己热衷于每一个场合,做好每一次演讲。所以我总是能够对每一个社团产生兴趣,并能利用当地人最熟悉的例证来阐述我那些最简单的道理。

  按照我平时的习惯,这篇传记写到此也该就此结束了,但是在最后我真挚并虔诚地希望这本书能够在今后继续为世界各国的人们带来帮助。

鲁塞·康维尔

马萨诸塞,南华盛顿

1913 年 9 月 1 日